*Subtitle:* **THE SECRET TO BOLDER IDEAS, BIGGER BETS, AND CREATIVE BREAKTHROUGHS**

BIS Publishers
Timorplein 46
1094 CC Amsterdam
The Netherlands
T +31 (0)20 515 02 30
bis@bispublishers.com
www.bispublishers.com
ISBN 978 90 636 9726 6
Copyright © 2024 Brendan Kearns and BIS Publishers.

*Title:*

# EVERYTHING IS A PROTOTYPE

**BRENDAN KEARNS** *(author)*

**BIS**

# CONSEQUENCES 85

# EXPERIMENTATION 121

# ITERATION 193

# AUTHOR'S NOTE

Too many people spend a large portion of their lives avoiding mistakes at all costs, searching for familiar answers to new questions, unaware of being trapped in a mental prison of their own making. Nowhere is this more evident than in our blindness to our most innate capacity: the everyday use of our creativity.

Before you dive in, there are two things I want to share about this book:

1. **It's designed to be a practical, no-nonsense guide to creativity**—grounded in experience and stripped of the self-indulgence that sometimes sneaks into books like this. If you've ever felt let down by promises of transformation that left you unchanged, this one is meant to deliver something different. Every page is the product of my obsession with the power of human ingenuity—crafted to be useful, economical, and worth your time.

2. **This book uses stories as a frame for its practical tools.** You'll encounter moments from my own life and the lives of others that are meant to inspire and guide you, but I know not everyone reads the same way. Some of you may love the stories, while others might prefer to jump straight to the actionable parts. That's okay. The book is designed

to support both approaches, with clear visual cues and section markers so you can find what you need. Whether you choose to follow the narrative flow or dip into specific tools, the ideas here are meant to meet you where you are.

I've never liked the saying, "There's no such thing as a bad idea." There are bad ideas—not because they fail, but because they're careless or even harmful. Take my own teenage misadventure with a speargun in a garden pond, which cost me a tooth and a good deal of pride. It was a foolish idea, yes, but it taught me the difference between mistakes we can learn from and ones we're better off avoiding.

This book isn't about judging ideas by their moral weight. It's about making space to pursue ideas with purpose, then shaping, testing, and refining them. It's about cultivating the mindset to bring ideas into the world and see if they stand on their own merit. If you're willing to prototype enough ideas, I promise you'll eventually uncover ones that truly matter.

So how do we turn our ideas into action without risking more than we can afford? The tools in these pages are here to help you sidestep the traps of modern life and work that stifle creativity and ingenuity. My aim is to empower you to have, make, build, and share ideas relentlessly. Because even if most of those ideas don't work, the act of trying will lead you somewhere remarkable. And when you get there, it will be a beautiful thing.

— Brendan

# INTRODUCTION
*A Crisis of Playing It Safe*

"Caution is the path to mediocrity. Gliding, passionless mediocrity is all that most people think they can achieve."

FRANK HERBERT

# TWO BAKERS

Nestled between a dusty hardware store and a dry cleaner on a busy high street in North London is an abandoned shopfront. On its door hangs a sign from a local real estate agent, promising a 'unique retail opportunity' and 'ample foot traffic.' A little over a year ago it was the home of a budding new bakery. Today it's empty and deserted.

Its previous tenant, Jack, had always dreamed of opening his own bakery. He'd learned everything about running one for the last 10 years—working his way up from dogsbody to baker's apprentice to manager. When he walked past the shopfront on his way home from work one day, the sign stopped him dead in his tracks. He'd made this same journey hundreds of times and always imagined one of the shops on this street being his own. Staring through the window, he could see it all come to life. He imagined polished wooden countertops, assortments of delicious treats, the smell of fresh ground coffee, the hiss of steaming milk, and rows upon rows of fresh sourdough, baguette, and brioche. A few weeks later, he took his £10,000 in savings and a £40,000 loan from the bank and signed a two-year lease on the building. The vision of Jack's Bakery was born.

Over the next eight weeks, Jack worked tirelessly on the fit-out of his new store. He hired carpenters, electricians, painters, and even convinced a well-known graphic designer to do the branding. With a small team of casual sales staff, he opened the doors a little over two months later. Jack's Bakery was in business.

Sales were slow in the beginning. Initially, he blamed it on a spike in wet weather and the train station across the road being closed for renovations. As he'd been counting on attracting hungry commuters, he told himself that it was just a hiccup, things would get better once the station reopened.

A week or two later, with the weather improving and an influx of passing commuters thanks to the re-opening of the train station, sales still didn't improve. After a few more weeks, still nothing. Very quickly, Jack had to let go of some of his casual staff. To be fair, they were spending most of their time pretending to be busy anyway.

After three months, Jack's bank balance was getting dangerously low. He did everything he could think of to get more customers: changed the type of snacks he sold in the morning; introduced a loyalty scheme; offered discounts; he even gave away free coffee vouchers to tired commuters, trying to entice them into his now struggling business. None of it helped. He was barely making enough money to cover expenses, let alone make a living.

Late one night, Jack did the numbers and realised that he only had enough left for two more months of rent, loan repayments, and supplies. The writing was on the wall. Jack had no choice. In less than six months, he'd spent tens of thousands of pounds and his dream was all but dead. He would be left with nothing.

Lisa didn't know Jack but she'd watched him go out of business. A pastry chef by trade, she loved seeing someone doing what she'd always dreamt of. When she heard Jack was shutting down, she wondered what had gone wrong. She always had her professional opinion about what could've been done better, but she never imagined Jack's Bakery would go out of business in six months. It didn't make sense. They were in a great location, so she thought, and the shop looked fantastic. When she shared her thoughts with one of her friends, they made an off-hand comment about her being just as qualified to run it as anyone else. This got her thinking...maybe she could make it work? Maybe she could do it better. Maybe this was the opportunity she was looking for? After all, the shop was already fitted out with everything she needed to open a bakery.

Lisa called the real estate agent a few days later, half curious and half hoping for a good deal, given that Jack had gone out of business and left the landlord without a paying tenant. Annoyingly, the agent said that the owner wasn't willing to rent it to anyone for less than a two year minimum and a sizable deposit. Once bitten, twice shy, she guessed. Two years was longer than Lisa was willing to commit to the idea so she let it go, for a while. But the idea was seeded. After a series of late nights browsing commercial real estate listings for alternative locations and a lot of back-of-a-napkin planning, Lisa stumbled across a company that rented out specialised retail space by the day. You could run a coffee pop-up in central London on Monday, a cafe for the creatives in Shoreditch on Tuesday, and another for the old money crowd in Kensington on Wednesday. All without a two year contract.

The idea of not being locked-in to a long-term lease got Lisa thinking; why not test the idea for her bakery before committing to it full time? Instead of quitting her job and going all-in, she could rent a new location for a couple of days to see if it was worth the risk.

And so Lisa went about her experiment. She rented a new space every Saturday in different neighbourhoods. Instead of spending hours baking each week, she arranged to buy her stock wholesale from someone else. She even roped in friends and family as cheap labour in her pop-up bakeries while she was building up her confidence (and cash reserves to hire some weekend staff.)

In less than a month, Lisa had created a system that would allow her to run temporary bakeries all across London, all without the risk of hinging everything on the one location. She avoided the stress of committing to long-term leases and the financial risk that goes with them. This gave her time to focus on other questions: Was her dream of opening her own bakery a viable idea? Was it more viable in the north, east, west, or south parts of the city? And if she went full-time on her new business, which location made the most sense?

Lisa is what I call a *Prototyper*. Instead of assuming that there was only one way of setting up a bakery, she did what all good prototypers do—experiment. Instead of taking over Jack's lease and committing to a fixed location, she took her idea and found a way to test it in different neighbourhoods. She had ideas, found a way to test them, made mistakes, and learned how to make small changes each time based on what she'd learned (which we'll learn more about in the Iteration chapter later in this book). Instead of spending the early hours of every weekend baking, she bought her stock from someone else to test different kinds of breads and pastries, cakes, macaroons, cookies, and more. She carefully tracked how many people came into her pop-ups, what sold in different neighbourhoods, the busiest times of the day, and the different store layouts that turned over the most customers. Of course, it goes without saying that she made mistakes. But she made them cheaply. She learned quickly that three baristas on weekdays in the city and extra waitstaff in the suburbs on a weekend made everyone's life a lot easier, and made her a lot more money. In the same amount of time that Jack opened and closed his bakery (6 months), Lisa had perfected hers. She'd done it experimentally, allowed herself room for drastic changes, and did it all at a fraction of the cost.

Prototyping gave Lisa the feedback she needed to be more certain about the kind of bakery she would eventually open and where it was most likely to be successful. She removed the stress and uncertainty that comes with going all-in, like Jack did, and gave herself an edge over someone trying to do the same thing the "conventional" way. In a strange twist of fate, months after Jack was forced to close, the landlord that refused to rent their shop for less than two years finally listed his space with the same company that Lisa used to run her pop-ups. She had an opportunity to set up shop there for one Saturday only. And so, sandwiched between a dusty hardware store and a dry cleaner on a busy north London high street, Lisa learned with a prototype in one day the same lesson that cost Jack his life savings...it was a terrible location for a bakery.

# A BETTER WAY TO SOLVE PROBLEMS

This isn't a book about how to open a bakery or run a business. This is a field guide for having better ideas and how to test them. It's about untangling how we're taught to judge our thinking against a rigid criteria of right and wrong, good and bad, and the debilitating effect this has on our capacity for innovative problem solving every day.

Over the next few chapters, I'm going to teach you how to think and behave more experimentally about everything from sport to side hustles, your career, and even parts of your personal life. Along the way, you'll develop a fool proof method of using your creativity to bring your ideas to life, and learn how to make course corrections when necessary. By the end of this book, you'll be a Prototyper. You'll take big risks in a more manageable way—with structure, self-compassion, and objectivity, which are all key ingredients to worthwhile creativity of any kind.

Above all else, I'm going to teach you how to make better mistakes by making them cheaply and relatively risk-free. You'll also learn how to make better decisions by sorting the wheat from the chaff. This is an integral reminder, because ultimately— the most successful companies and people in the world have learned that while mistakes are a cost of doing business, the wisest use it as fuel for growth. Having gone through the gauntlet of companies like Google and Twitter myself, I've seen first-hand the power of understanding and celebrating your biggest cockups. It leads to better work, bigger breakthroughs, and more innovative ideas. Not to mention a better way to spend your time. However, it takes more than just airing your mistakes to make them useful. First you have to understand why we make them.

# A NOTE ON PERFECTIONISM

Perfectionism has a strange reputation. On the one hand, it's an admirable trait. She's a real perfectionist, they say. It demands the very best—never settles. No room for compromise. While on the other hand, it's debilitating. It is an impossible standard that can never be met. Oh, stop being such a perfectionist, they also say. Where it's relevant to us is when it leads us down the wrong path—when we're so fixated on avoiding failure that we're blind to the ignorance this creates.

In some ways, despite his failure, Jack could be called a Perfectionist. Before opening his bakery, everything had to be just right. There had to be polished countertops, beautiful graphics, and an abundance of bubbly staff. He had an image in his head of what a real bakery should look like and how it operated, and he went about recreating it: Find a space, sign a lease, fitout the store, hire a team, open the doors, start baking, and hope for the best. This way of thinking is what's known as the Einstellung Effect*. It's a rigidness, or blindness, to better ways of solving problems because we're so predisposed to solving them in a certain way, even when there are better

---

* The Einstellung Effect: The tendency to revert to methods that are familiar, even when there's a better way of solving a problem. We fail to see it because of how experience shapes our thinking.

alternatives available.

If Jack had been successful, it's more than likely that instead of criticising his perfectionism, we'd be telling his story very differently. Instead of combing over every decision for blame, we'd credit them for his success. We might even call it something else: visionary, vigilant; or committed. The problem here is what's known as Survivor Bias—a psychological flaw that leads us to attribute the success of something to an otherwise meaningless trait (like combing your hair from right to left) merely because it's visible in the successes we can see. And it affects all of us more than we realise.

We all have a blindness when it comes to solving problems, even as experts. Or more precisely, because we're experts. Despite Jack's experience, he couldn't turn his idea into a successful business. There was a way to do it, Lisa proved that. But Jack had never started a business before, he'd only worked in someone else's. He based all of his decisions on the information he had available. He followed a known template—approaching the challenge the only way he knew how, the way everyone else did. And he created a situation where he would be left with nothing if he was wrong. This is a wrong kind of mistake.

My goal in writing this book is to help you make the right mistakes. To repair your relationship with creativity as a tool for exploration, and guide you through productive ways to use it to your advantage by learning how to make mistakes in the right way. What's a "right" mistake, you might be thinking? They're those we make intentionally to test a hypothesis about the world—like a scientist experimenting on their way to greater discovery. After all, mistakes and failure are a critical ingredient to any innovative process.

For now, trust me that this book, with a little experimentation of your own, will help you find the techniques and approaches that work best for you, so that bad ideas and ineffective routines can be weeded out to create room for something better.

This book is organised into six themes that have emerged in my practice. Part 1 (Permission) explores the question of whether we are born with a fear of failure or if it's acquired as we grow up, go to school, and enter the world of work—and asks what we can do about it. Part 2 (Vulnerability) introduces us to accountability and the power of thinking and failing openly, and why it's so hard to do after decades of being told it should be avoided at all costs. Part 3 (Consequences) looks at the feedback and punishment we receive for our mistakes, whether they're mild or severe, public or private, internal or external. It also explores the social, physical, and financial consequences of failing. Part 4 (Experimentation) teaches you how to become a Prototyper—introducing a way of leaning into mistakes more intentionally as a method to pursue progress. Using examples from sports, popular culture, design, and business, it will teach you how to create and run experiments of your own. Finally, Part 5 (Iteration) and Part 6 (Resilience) prepare you for what to do with the results of your experiments, what you've discovered, and how to know whether to keep going or if it's time to stop. These are the processes and values I strive to cultivate in my own life and work. It's my hope that the methods inside this book will be a foundation for similarly chaotic minds to do the same.

There's a story from the height of WW2 that's often used, maybe overused, to describe *Survivor Bias*. The US military was trying to reduce the number of American planes shot down over Europe. At the time, they knew that they needed to do more to protect planes and their crew, but making any aircraft invincible would also make it almost impossible to fly.

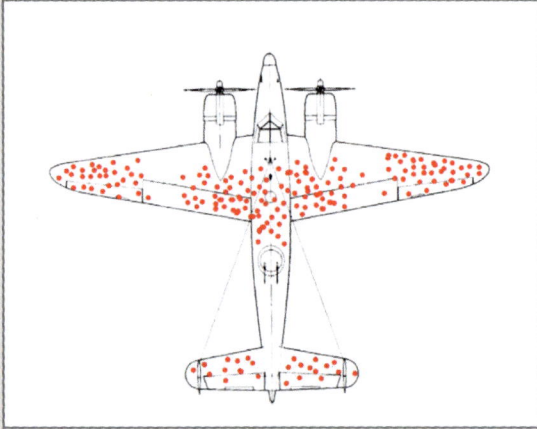

Fig 1: Damage recorded to places returning from recent missions

According to the data they had at the time, planes returning from their missions recorded most damage on the fuselage, tail, and wings (*Fig 1*). Analysts initially suggested adding armour to these areas to make more planes more likely to survive their missions. While logical from a data perspective, Hungarian statistician Dr. Abraham Wald realised a fatal flaw. The data came from damage reports that only included planes that returned safely from their missions. Planes that received the worst damage—the kind that needed to be reinforced against—were missing from the data because they never made it back to base to have their damage recorded. Instead, they were twisted piles of metal scattered across Europe.

Just like Jack believing that foot traffic would all but guarantee the success of his bakery, analysts couldn't see the full picture because the cause of failures weren't visible. And they almost made a horrendous mistake because of it.

Instead of adding armour to the body, tail, and wings, Wald suggested adding it to areas of surviving planes that had little or no damage at all (*Fig* 2). Most notably the engines and cockpit. Wald's revelation is an example of being aware of the potential for making flawed conclusions because you can't see the full picture. Like missing data, Survivor Bias is a blind spot to what failure can teach us, mostly because we can't see it.

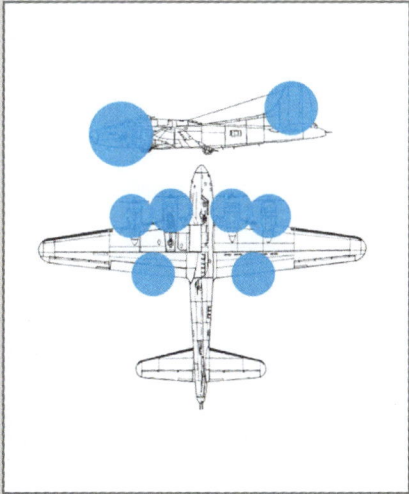

Fig 2: Wald's final recommendation on where to add extra armour

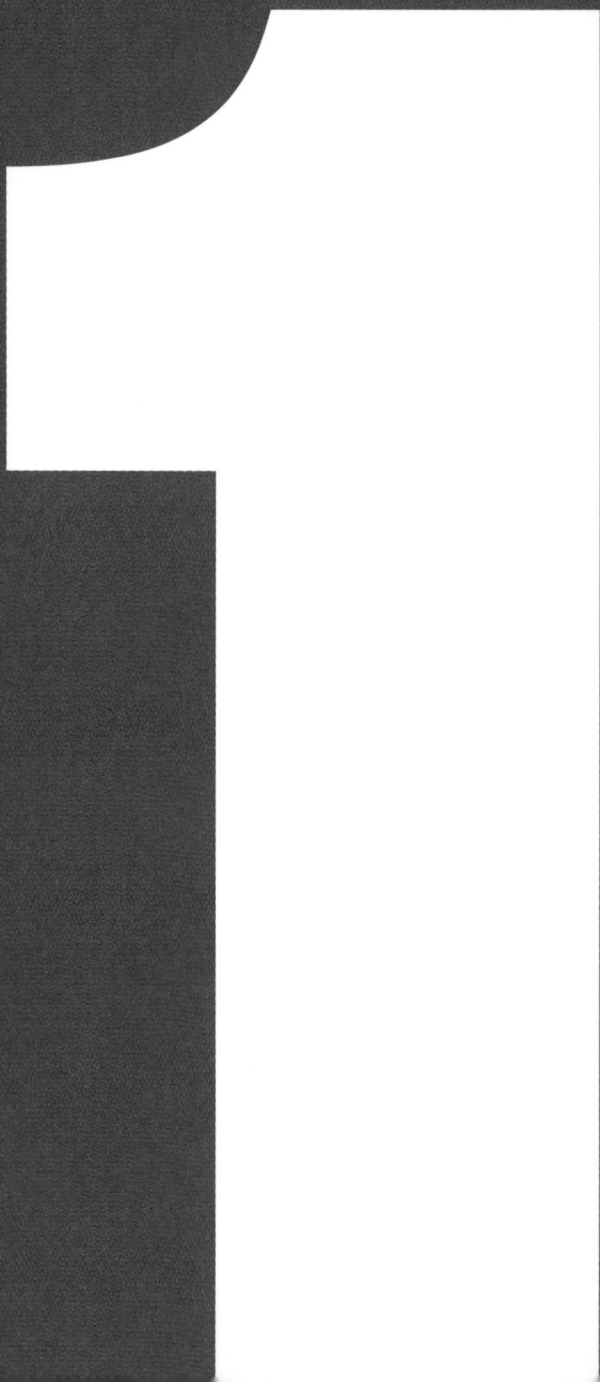

Reclaiming the Right to Try

# PERM
# ISS
# ION

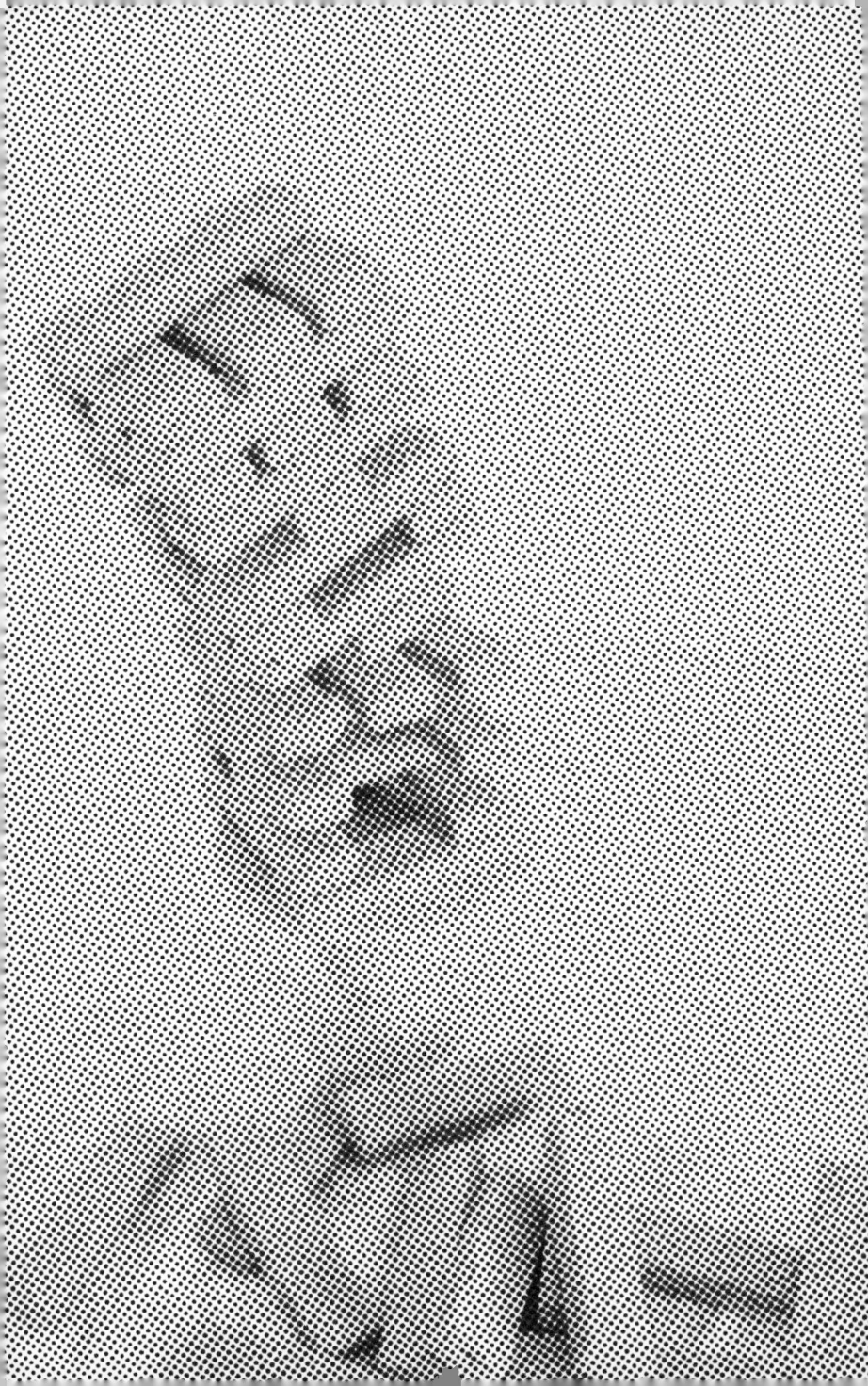

# THE FOUR YEAR OLD GENIUS

"If I had to live my life again, I'd make
the same mistakes, only sooner."

TALLULAH BANKHEAD

In 2006, Jack Skillman walked on stage at the TED conference in Monterey, California. He explained how with twenty pieces of uncooked spaghetti, some string, and a single marshmallow, you could learn a lot about how people solve problems and the downside of how we're taught to do so in the modern world.

The goal of Skillman's experiment is simple: Teams of four are asked to build the tallest structure they can in eighteen minutes and the group with the tallest tower wins. There is only one rule: the marshmallow must go on top.

Skillman has run the Marshmallow Tower Challenge with hundreds of people of all ages, from executives to engineers, from Tokyo to Silicon Valley. As you'd expect, people in technical jobs like engineering do quite well. If they didn't, I'd be worried about taking a meeting on the upper floors of an office building or driving across a bridge. But there's one part of Skillman's story that always catches people's attention. By every measure, one group always outperforms the rest: Kindergarteners. It doesn't matter what adults do for a living, children as young as four build towers that are taller and more stable than any other group. Most people expect four-year olds to descend into chaos. I know I did. However, the opposite is true.

When you compare the results of kindergarteners to those of business school students, things get even more interesting. It doesn't matter if business students attend the most prestigious universities in the world—children are more capable of building a taller, more stable tower with the same instructions, time limit, and raw materials. If you observe the two groups, you couldn't pick two more different approaches to the same challenge.

Skillman's business students start with a formal meeting to talk over the details. They ask questions like: Who's in charge? What's the end goal? What are the constraints? What role do I play? As the challenge goes on and they realise that they're running out of time, they quickly assemble a makeshift tower and spike the marshmallow on its highest point. Having spent so much time in debate, the tower often collapses under its weight as the buzzer sounds. As you might expect, people often start to look for someone to blame. They go into a ritual of self-preservation, turning on each other to protect their reputations. This might feel very familiar.

Meanwhile, on the kindergartners table, something completely different is happening. There are no strategy meetings; no scrambling for the gavel; no delegation, nor hierarchies to make decisions on behalf of the group. As

Skillman said, "kindergarteners don't argue who's going to be CEO of Spaghetti Inc." They get on with honest, messy work. They manhandle the materials to understand their dexterity—examining how things work together. They break the spaghetti, squeeze the marshmallow, and cut the tape. Some decide to work together as a team while others work alone, often venturing off to explore an idea before coming back and interrupting everyone to share what they've learned. When I spoke to Skillman in late 2020, he was still convinced that the reason children did better than all the other groups was because they didn't participate in what he called "status transactions," that is, games of hierarchy, dominance, and ego. All of which lead to worse results.

By all accounts, children build taller, more stable towers by understanding the constraints of their materials and learning through failure and iteration, whereas business students fall into a trap of hypothesising the perfect outcome using the limited understanding they already have. Kindergarteners will "prototype" dozens of half-baked ideas, most of them terrible, before arriving at a feasible one. Whereas adults, as Skillman says, "often accept the rules as sacrosanct and don't challenge them." It makes sense when you think about the modern workplace and people's experience with things like performance anxiety, perfectionism, and procrastination. Unlike adults, kindergarteners are not paralysed by analysis or shrouded in shame at the likelihood of mistakes. They haven't learned that yet. They fail and iterate accordingly—never even noticing the mistakes as anything other than stepping stones.

For too many of us, the attraction of perfectionism is

also the cause of our paralysis. Everything grinds to a halt in the search for finding the perfect answer to a question, or the right solution to a problem, and when we can't, our focus shifts to that of our survival. Children, on the other hand, aren't plagued with the same anxiety about being wrong, at least not yet. My question is, why do we lose this as we grow up? Why are preschoolers able to navigate this while business school students, with all their study and experience, are some of the worst performers of all?

By default, perfectionism and safety have become the way by which most of us operate in the world. We go to school, start careers, and do work that reinforces the same messages: do not colour outside the lines; there is no room for error here. One might think this would foster productivity, which is understandable if you think about society as a production line. But we're not. Most of us are in search of novel answers to new problems every day, not a more efficient way of doing the same thing as before.

# THE DECLINE OF
# NATURAL CREATIVITY

"What we have concluded is that
non-creative behaviour is learned."

DR GEORGE LAND

In the 1960s, NASA approached researchers George Land and Beth Jarman with a question: How can we find the most creative people in our ranks? At the time, the space agency was looking for the brightest minds to work on its biggest challenges—most notably rocketing a small crew of astronauts a few hundred thousand miles to the moon and back. The problem for Land and Jarman was that despite decades of research into creative imagination, there wasn't a universal test to measure it in people. So they designed one. The test was designed to measure what's called *Divergent Thinking*—the ability to see a problem and find multiple solutions. It's pretty simple. When you're asked a question with many possible answers, the more answers you can imagine, the more creative you're likely to be. And it worked, at least for finding the most creative rocket scientists.

Land and Jarman's test worked so well as a way of scoring divergent thinking that after its success at finding hidden talent inside NASA, they decided to run it with an even more challenging group of people than rocket scientists: Children.

The results from the first group of 1,800 children they tested, aged just five years old, found something remarkable. The number of children that scored at 'genius' levels of creativity was 98%. Let that sink in for a second. Ninety. Eight. Percent. Impressed, they decided to extend the study. When the same group of kids were tested five years later at the age of ten, the number that scored at genius levels dropped to just 30%. By the age of fifteen, it was as low as 12%.

When the same test was done with over 200,000 adults in a broader study, the scores were a dismal 2%. What does this say about how we nurture our innate talent for creativity and innovative thinking? How prepared are we with the tools we need to succeed in the world? As Land put it, "What we have concluded is that non-creative behaviour is learned."

## PERCENTAGE OF "GENIUS" LEVEL RESULTS IN DIVERGENT THINKING BY AGE

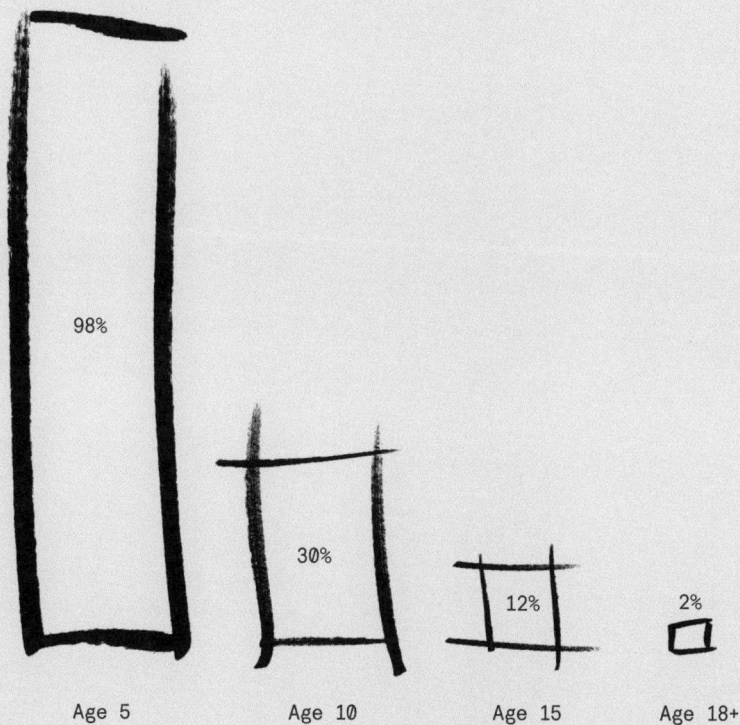

98%

30%

12%

2%

Age 5          Age 10          Age 15          Age 18+

# IT STARTS AT HOME

Imagine this scenario: You're twelve years old and you've just come home from school with a bad grade on a science test. When you show your parents, do they:

A : Express anger or disappointment, making it clear you've really messed up;

B : Sit you down and ask you what happened and what you're going to do differently next time; or

C : Hug you and tell you not to worry because you're still good at other subjects.

Some people have had (or been) the parent that opts for *Option A* at one time or another. And while *Option C* is the kindest, *Option B* is most likely to teach a child that failure isn't catastrophic and that their ability is something that can be improved over time.

Stanford psychologists Kyla Haimovitz and Carol Dweck published a study that found that parents who treat failure and mistakes as some kind of debilitating experience will often raise children who believe that they can't get any smarter—that intelligence and ability is fixed. As a result, many people grow up convinced that they have little control over their abilities and are more likely to view mistakes as a sign to give up, or worse, never try in the first place, instead of an opportunity to learn from and do better next time. There has been further research that found that people who believe that *intelligence* is malleable are not just more aware of the potential for screw ups in the first place, but recover faster and learn more from them when they do happen. It turns out a lot of our permission to make mistakes (and the ability to benefit from them) is determined by the mindset we learn at home.

In the end, it's fair to say that education, for all its flaws, isn't entirely to blame for our collective fear of failure. Our parents and our home environments have a huge influence over how we perceive and react to mistakes. But don't be too hard on them, their parents probably did the same thing, and so on. And without knowing it, you might be doing it to the next generation.

Everything is a Prototype

# PERFECTION REALLY IS THE ENEMY

In their book Art & Fear, David Bayles and Ted Orland tell the story of a ceramics teacher turning her students into unsuspecting lab rats to see whether focusing on quality or quantity produced the best work. Her experiment was brilliant in its simplicity.

At the start of the semester, the ceramics teacher divided her students into two groups. The first group were told that their final grade would depend on the **number** of ceramic pots they produced *(Quantity)*. At the same time, the second group were told that their grade would be based on a **single** piece of work, entirely of their choosing *(Quality)*.

The two groups toiled throughout the semester with their instructions, one group turning over hundreds of pots while the other group focused on creating a single masterpiece. On the last day of class, both groups presented their work. As Bayles and Orland observed:

> "The works of the highest quality were all produced by the group being graded for quantity. It seems that while the quantity group was busily churning out piles of work, the quality group had sat theorising about perfection, and in the end had little more to show for their efforts than grandiose theories and a pile of dead clay."

It appears that our business school graduates in Skillman's marshmallow tower experiment aren't alone. But what does this mean in terms of changing how you solve problems? To do that we have to break down what's happening in both examples.

When it comes to solving any problem, learning through mistakes and iteration will get you further than speculating over the perfect outcome. Unfortunately for most of us, we think and work in a way that doesn't cultivate a safe environment for making mistakes. But it doesn't have to be that way.

The first thing to recognise is time. Or more precisely, that a challenge generally takes place within a fixed amount of it. Skillman's marshmallow towers had to be built in 18 minutes. The ceramics students had a full semester. But in both cases they were working within a fixed amount of it.

But for now, I want to focus on the other thing that's happening in these examples. It's more subtle, although very visible once you know what to look out for—and it's the most powerful thing of all. It's the mechanics of how we think. And we use this process as a way of making decisions every day.

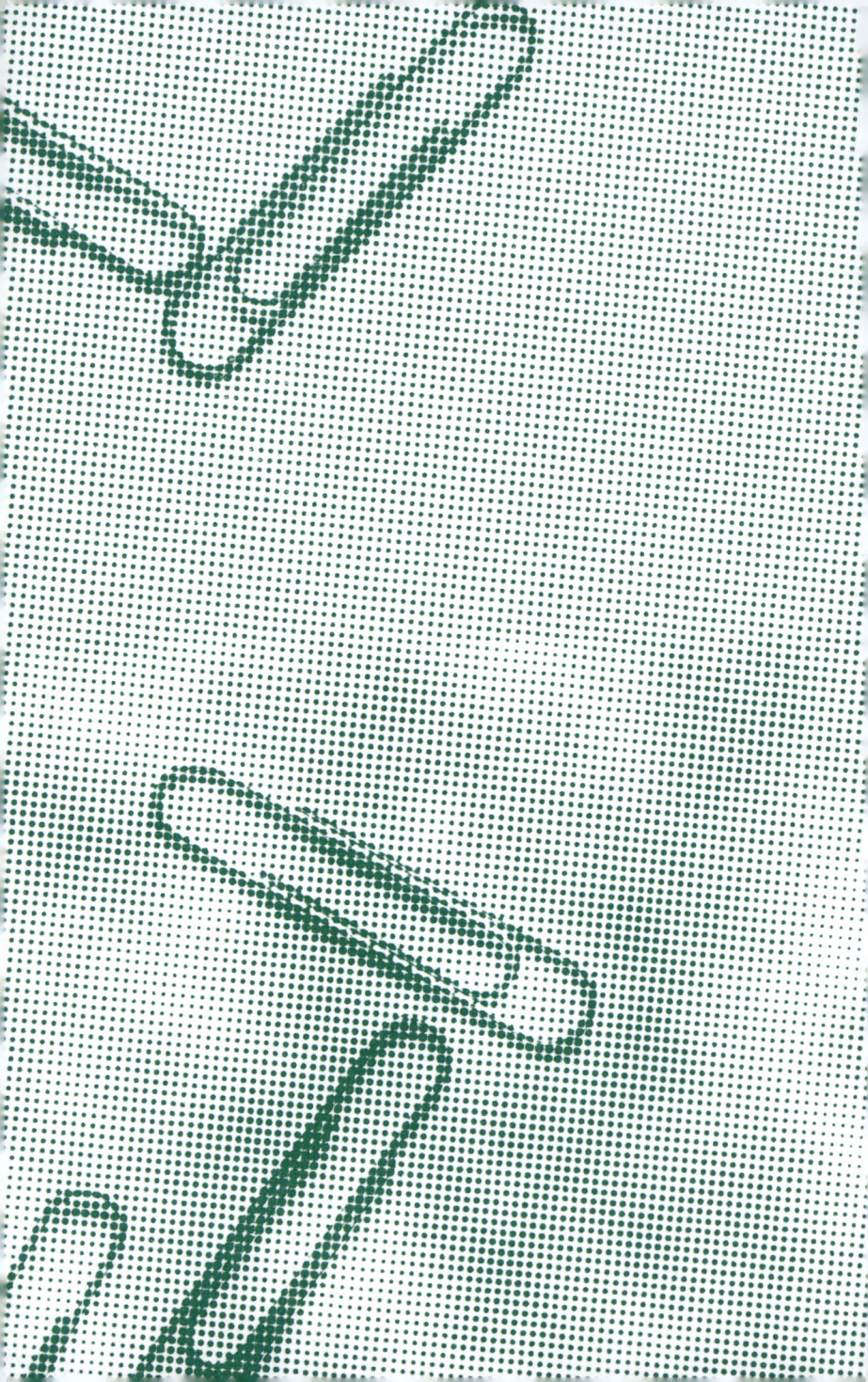

# HOW MANY WAYS CAN YOU USE A PAPERCLIP?

Broadly speaking, there are two modes of creative thinking: *Divergent* and *Convergent*. Divergent thinking is the process of coming up with as many ideas as possible in response to a question. For example, how many uses can you think of for a paperclip? Five? Ten? One thousand? It's also viewing the question from different perspectives, e.g. can the paperclip be the size of a bus? What if it's made out of styrofoam and floats on water?

A few years ago, I was on the phone with a recruiter from a tech company when she asked, "What's the best way to design an elevator system in a building that's 10,000 floors tall?" This is the kind of brain-teaser that's designed to see how a candidate thinks, not necessarily whether they know the right answer or not. (I said I'd turn the building on its side and build a road alongside it. That way you wouldn't need a complicated elevator system. The recruiter wasn't impressed. But you can't win them all...)

Divergent and convergent thinking are potent tools for creativity and problem solving but, like oil and water, they don't mix. Think back to the kindergarteners and business school graduates in the Marshmallow Tower Challenge. If I asked you which group was being divergent and which was convergent, could you tell? Who was trying to find as many potential solutions as possible? And who was searching for the right solution in a list of options? It's easy to say that the kindergarteners were divergent while the business grads were convergent, which is almost true. In reality, they were both using divergent and convergent thinking, only the business school grads were using them both **at the same time**—killing their ability to build the tallest tower because they were sacking ideas as they appeared with all the reasons they wouldn't work, instead of creating a number of options before committing to one that looked the most promising.

Try to remember a situation where you were told to "*be creative.*" As someone who's worked in creative jobs for over 15 years, the instruction still gives me anxiety. Usually (in a business or work setting) it involves a group of people in a meeting, trying to find answers to a problem. When it happens, before you've spoken a word or written anything down, have you ever found yourself putting your thoughts through a critical process in your head? Have you ever found enough mental evidence that it might not work and decided that it's best not to share it with the group? Or worse, if you do share it, have you been told that "it'll never work," "we've tried that before," or even "that's a crazy idea"? That's Convergence creeping in, as both a behaviour and a mindset, when it's least useful. Over my career I've experienced many times the chasm between good and bad ideas. In fact, I'd go as far as saying that most ideas aren't great. But trying to be divergent under conditions of convergence is like trying to save a sinking ship by bailing out water one teaspoon at a time. It feels like you're doing a lot of work, but it's not very effective.

By now you might be thinking that it's all well and good to fail and make mistakes when you have permission. But what if you don't? What if you're unsure about ideas as they appear, and find it hard to see or judge their value?

—

When I worked at a big tech company, one of my managers was a real piece of work. The kind who could turn a room tense with a single comment. He had a knack for projecting his toxic traits onto our team, making it painfully clear that being wrong wasn't an option. Meetings became exercises in survival. No one dared to speak, breathe, or even move.

As designers, it was our job to come up with new ways to solve problems—to push the boundaries of what was possible (and sometimes what felt impossible). But doing this inside a global tech company means the stakes are high. A small mistake can quickly become a big one, visible to billions of people. To do our jobs well, we needed open, honest feedback sessions. These are known as critiques, or 'crits' and are a common ritual in design and tech teams. It's about presenting ideas, prototypes, and research, then inviting colleagues to find the weak spots so we can make them stronger.

But under this manager's influence, critique turned into a blood sport. The space for honest feedback evaporated, replaced by a game of who can stay out of the line of fire. The months I worked for him were a blur of anxiety. Every time I got into the elevator and took it to the 4th floor of the office, I felt knots in my stomach. Even after meetings, I'd replay every word: Had I said too much? Too little? Was my job on the line?

Our environment was riddled with passive aggression, tension, and uncertainty. It felt like a nerdy episode of Survivor, just with fewer abs and more presentations. We weren't collaborating; we were just trying to survive. We were victims of badly timed convergence. Forced decisions and conclusions at every turn. Unsurprisingly, our work suffered for it.

Whenever I tell this story, people react with shock. The kinds of big tech companies I've worked for are supposed to be playgrounds for nerds. A place where people are free to be their best selves, showered in perks and permission. But my experience was a reminder that even in the most permissive environments, a single toxic person can silence our greatest creative capacities.

And worst of all, it can reinforce the fear that keeps so many people from speaking up or taking risks—the fear of making *mistakes.*

# PERMISSION TO INCUBATE

Former Madison Avenue advertising executive Charles Brower once said that "a new idea is delicate. It can be killed by a sneer or a yawn; it can be stabbed to death by a joke, or worried to death by a frown on the right person's brow." I think he was right. And not just about the fragility of taglines to sell toothpaste or sugary drinks. It's true about anything new, uncertain, and untested.

The easiest thing to do when faced with a budding idea is to find all of the reasons it might not work, or worse, kill it with judgement before it's had the chance to see the light of day. There's an example I like to use to bring this to life:

Imagine that I gave you two eggs. Both identical in size, colour, and weight. Now imagine that I asked you to tell me which egg was most likely to hatch into a healthy young chick and which is destined to be a life unrealised. What would you say your chances are of picking correctly? Unless you're a poultry farmer, your odds are likely to be 50/50.

The fragility of new ideas means that without giving them time to prove their worth, or lack of worth, before throwing them away, there's almost no way to see their true potential. In contrast, allowing multiple ideas time to mature is a guaranteed way of finding out which has the greater chance of success. I call this process Incubation, and we'll learn more about the step-by-step process in the Experimentation chapter later in the book. For now, I want to focus on the most fundamental part of being experimental—the permission to do it in the first place.

When it comes to new ideas and making mistakes, the first step in permission is to recognise that the fear of consequences is mostly acquired, taught over many years, and reinforced by the structures and institutions around you. My challenge—and the entire purpose of this book—is to confront the notion that you're powerless to change it. If you've ever heard yourself say, *"Yes, but . . ."* or *"That won't work because…"* in response to your own ideas or someone else's, then you might have a convergence problem, and it's likely stifling the permission you need to make mistakes in the right way—as cheaply and frequently as possible.

# 2

# VULN ERA BILITY

In the Shadow of Criticism

# VULNERABILITY
# IN ACTION

"It is not the critic who counts; not the man who points out how the strong man stumbles, or where the doer of deeds could have done them better. The credit belongs to the man who is actually in the arena...who strives valiantly; who errs, who comes short again and again...his place shall never be with those cold and timid souls who neither know victory nor defeat."

THEODORE ROOSEVELT

On a cold Friday evening in March 2020, only a few weeks before the COVID pandemic locked us all in our homes, I was in a cosy pub for drinks with a dozen or so senior staffers from a financial aid charity. We'd just finished a day of workshops nearby and most of us were tired and looking forward to the weekend. The day itself was nothing out of the ordinary. It was the usual mix of team activities that you see in these kinds of 'away days.' Sometimes I think the reason people agree to attend them is just for an excuse to get away from the office.

I was speaking to one of the attendees, Maria, who confessed to feeling like an idiot for something she did earlier in the day. When I asked her why, she said she did something stupid when presenting her team's work in one of the activities. I couldn't remember her doing anything embarrassing, so I asked again and she explained. The activity she was referring to was straightforward. Everyone was told to form small groups of no more than four people and spend 15-20 minutes building a hypothesis for how they would solve one of three challenges:

1. How do we raise more money from donors?

2. How do we allocate funds to the right projects?

3. How do we measure the impact of those funds?

Maria was in the group tasked with the third question. In her day job at the charity, she was a fundraiser. She didn't have the expertise of some of her other colleagues on how to track how the money they raised affected people and issues on the ground. Nevertheless, she got to work.

At first, Maria said less than everyone else in her group. But after a few minutes, she loosened up and started adding her own ideas to the discussion. She asked other people for more information about their ideas and the conversation flowed until, surprisingly, time was up and everyone was asked to come back together. The facilitator then asked for volunteers from each group to stand up and give a general debrief of what they talked about, and even share some of the initial ideas they had in the exercise. Maria's group was first, and after no one put their hand up to volunteer, she stood up and began to speak.

Back in the pub, I asked Maria what it was she thought she'd said that made her feel like an idiot. My recollection was that the team's ideas were good. I particularly liked how, even though she didn't work on 'impact' areas for the charity in her day to day job, she leaned into the question and really brought a new *perspective*. Her reply was surprising. She said she felt like she'd devalued the work of her team and made herself look like a fool by admitting, in her own words, that she didn't have "the slightest bit of evidence that what I'm about to tell you is right or not." I reassured her it was nothing like that. Whether she believed me or not, I don't know.

Over the next hour, I spoke to a couple more people from the workshops and heard a similar story. Ben, the chief financial officer, laughed when I asked him about the day's activities, especially the moment when Maria presented her team's ideas. 'She was brave, wasn't she?' he said, taking a sip of his pint. 'I could never admit that openly. I'm always so paranoid about keeping up appearances, you know?' I asked him if he thought she'd come across as unprepared or foolish, and he raised an eyebrow, almost puzzled. "Oh, not at all. I thought she was pretty bold, actually. It's refreshing to see someone just say what they're thinking instead of pretending to be perfect. It shows a lot of character."

The conversation moved on to other topics, but the sentiment stuck with me. I spoke to Eleanor, who managed a different team at the charity. She, too, commented on Maria's moment in the workshop. 'When Maria stood up,' Eleanor said, 'it was like she was giving everyone else permission to just... try things out. I respect that kind of honesty. I mean, it made me feel like I could actually ask questions without seeming clueless.' She laughed, though quickly added, 'Not that I actually would, of course.'

I started to notice a pattern. Each person seemed to be holding themselves to a standard they didn't expect of others. They saw Maria's willingness to admit doubt and uncertainty not as a flaw but as a strength. Something that made her a little more human. And yet, when I asked if they could picture themselves doing the same, their responses were almost identical—grins, quick laughs, shakes of the head. Ben mentioned he felt like he'd be "eaten alive" if he showed any lack of confidence in his decisions. Eleanor talked about how her team "relies on her" for stability. To them, admitting an insecurity wasn't an option.

As the night wore on and people began to leave the pub, I couldn't help but reflect on the contradiction. Here was a group of intelligent, capable people, each doubting themselves, each admiring Maria's openness, yet unwilling to allow themselves the same latitude. They respected vulnerability in someone else, but feared it would cost them the respect of other people if they showed it personally.

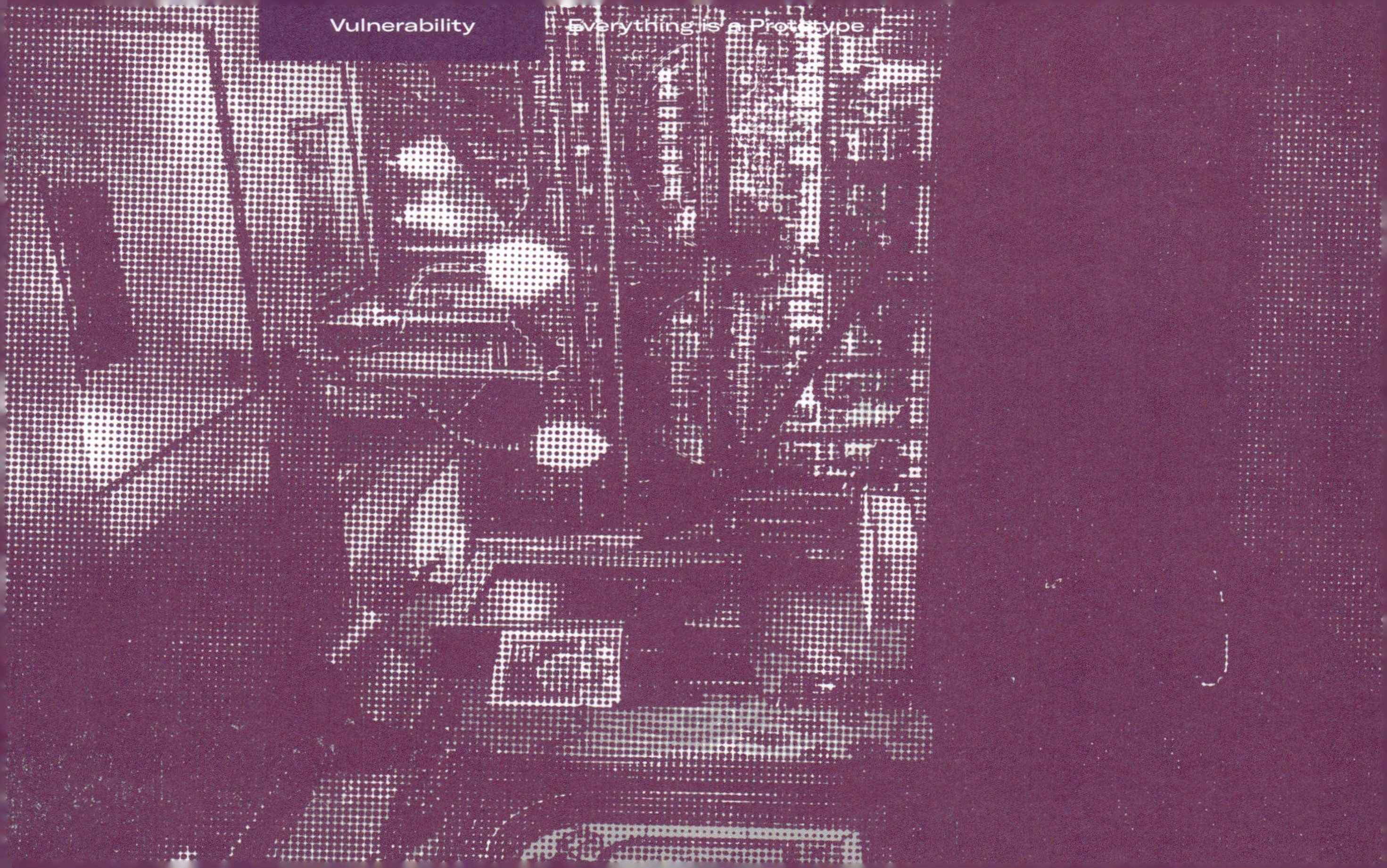

# PSYCHOLOGICAL EFFECTS
# OF VULNERABILITY

After the pub that night, I wondered what might happen if, just once, each of us leaned into that discomfort, if we dared to see in ourselves what we admired in Maria. Perhaps vulnerability only feels intimidating when it's our own. When we see it in someone else, it often appears courageous— even inspiring. Psychologists Anna Bruk and Sabine Scholl from the University of Mannheim call this the *Beautiful Mess Effect*. When we show signs of weakness, admit uncertainty, or make a mistake, we think we're exposing ourselves to judgement or criticism, as if revealing a flaw. However, when someone else does it, we often see it as something courageous, even admirable. What feels raw and exposing to us often appears brave and authentic to others.

When I say we "often" see it as courageous and admirable, I quite literally mean often. A classic study from the 1960s captures this well. Researchers showed participants videos of people spilling coffee during mock interviews. If viewers already perceived the person in the video as competent, the coffee spill was endearing—even positive. Showing small imperfections humanised them. But if the person in the video was seen as incompetent, their mistake had the opposite effect, making people doubt their abilities even more.

Even when she was nervous, Maria hadn't undermined

her credibility by saying she didn't know everything. Neither was she standing hunched over and speaking in a thin voice. She took up space and spoke confidently, while at the same time confessing she wasn't sure about the evidence behind what she was about to say. She humanised herself, which made her that much more approachable and grounded to her colleagues, and her colleagues more receptive to what she was saying. Generally, we overestimate how harshly we're judged when we show a weakness or doubt, and underestimate how much people will appreciate the honesty or courage it takes to reveal it.

This overestimation of how much others notice what we do is part of what's known as the *Spotlight Effect*. As if we walk around with a giant spotlight focused on our every move, highlighting every misstep and insecurity. Maria is a prime example. When she stood up to speak, she felt like every word was scrutinised, that any hesitation or uncertainty she showed would be judged. But the reality was different. Her colleagues hardly noticed the nerves she was sure were visible to everyone in the room. Whereas in reality, they admired her willingness to speak up, seeing her small admission of uncertainty as a strength, not a flaw.

The Spotlight Effect skews our perception. It makes us think that other people are as tuned into our inner thoughts and insecurities as we are. But most of the time, people are absorbed in their own concerns, rarely remembering our minor stumbles or imperfections as vividly as we do. This effect traps us in a distorted reality, where the fear of being noticed for our mistakes keeps us from expressing our ideas freely. It's a powerful illusion but, thankfully, only an illusion. By recognising the Spotlight Effect, we begin to release ourselves from the idea that we're always under scrutiny. We can approach our contributions with a bit more ease, knowing that others see far less than we think they do. And when they do notice, they often perceive our imperfections as a human quality worth admiring, not a reason to judge.

The Spotlight Effect is a paradox in psychology: In an effort to fit in, we monitor ourselves so closely that it creates a double bind. It's the constant need to belong and be accepted that ironically leads to the feeling of falling short. This distorted feedback loop makes us believe we're judged as harshly as we judge ourselves. We end up overcorrecting, or simply remaining silent, rather than taking a risk, speaking up, or showing our true selves.

Understanding the Spotlight Effect opens the door to a deeper insight: If we believe we're constantly under a watchful eye, then any feedback, criticism, or even advice can feel like proof that our worst fears are true. In Maria's case, she worried that even her admission of doubt would be seen as a sign of incompetence, something her colleagues would judge her by forever. This heightened self-consciousness can cause us to interpret even minor critiques as confirmation of our insecurities. But in the pub that night, Maria's openness was seen as brave and authentic by her colleagues. Their respect for her was confirmed, even strengthened, not damaged.

# SENSITIVITY TO CRITICISM: OUR SELF-PROTECTION THERMOSTAT

Imagine living in a world where no one ever asked for help or admitted anything less than total confidence. No one would express doubt, show visible signs of nerves, or share half-formed ideas until they were polished to perfection. It might sound far-fetched, but in a way, it's a world many of us already live in—not because it's required, but because we've come to treat criticism as a sign of weakness, a flaw in our abilities—or worse, in our character.

Criticism is a double-edged sword. On one hand, it's a powerful tool that can shine light on things we'd likely miss on our own. But it can also feel deeply personal, leaving us feeling defensive or uncertain. How we handle criticism is influenced by our sensitivity to it, like a thermostat setting that determines how we respond to feedback.

Until the early 1990s, research on how we react to criticism focused mainly on treating depression. But in 1994, Dr. Gordon Atlas set out to understand how people's sensitivity to criticism shaped their everyday lives. Observing people's emotional responses and behaviours in realistic settings, Atlas discovered something fascinating: people who were highly sensitive to criticism—who tended to feel it more deeply—were less motivated and showed reduced performance, especially under pressure. The greater someone's sensitivity, the more they risk falling into a cycle of self-doubt and defensiveness, sidetracking them from the task at hand and pulling them into the weeds of self-protection.

In many cases, vulnerability is perceived more positively than we expect. Yet our exaggerated sense of how others might judge us—compounded by our sensitivity to criticism—often prevent us from being open. Sensitivity to criticism is essentially a scale: it gauges how defensively we react or how personally we take feedback. Usually out of a fear that it reflects a fundamental flaw in us. A flaw that may or may not be fixable.

When we're sensitive to criticism, even helpful feedback can feel like a personal attack. The Spotlight Effect can intensify this response, making us believe others notice our weaknesses as sharply as we do. But as Maria's story shows, criticism—or even the possibility of it—can create a distorted feedback loop where we assume our mistakes are magnified in other people's eyes.

Sensitivity to criticism has a far-reaching impact on how we *think* and *behave*. While it doesn't necessarily stifle the imagination to create new things, it does make us less likely to pursue them if it means involving other people. After all, if we're too afraid to show something for fear of criticism, how can we ever be expected to refine our thinking, or muster the energy to think for ourselves in the first place?

**People with _higher_ sensitivity to criticism might:**

- Avoid sharing their ideas publicly
- React defensively, feel discouraged, or demotivated when receiving feedback
- Struggle to ask for help or admit when they don't know something
- Stick to "safe" ideas rather than proposing something new

**People with _lower_ sensitivity to criticism might:**

- Actively seek feedback on their ideas and work
- View feedback and setbacks as an opportunity for growth and learning
- Be willing to admit mistakes and learn from them
- Take calculated risks and propose innovative ideas

# UNDERSTANDING YOUR SENSITIVITY TO CRITICISM

Before we can learn to embrace criticism, we need to understand our relationship with it. The *Sensitivity to Criticism Scale* by Dr. Atlas offers a way to gauge how we respond to criticism, helping us pinpoint where we might be holding back. The scale isn't about labelling someone as *"too sensitive"* or *"not sensitive enough."* Instead, it's about understanding how sensitivity to criticism might be influencing behaviours and decisions. We all sit somewhere on the spectrum of sensitivity, affecting how we share ideas, respond to feedback, or take risks.

I've taken similar tests over the years, and I find that the results can change over time. My reaction to feedback in the past might not be the same today. In the same way, your results are likely to vary too. Chances are that simply becoming aware of your sensitivity to criticism will shift how you react to it from now on. Or, at least, highlight where you're starting from.

The tool I've put here is not Dr Atlas' official Sensitivity to Criticism Scale. Instead, there are a series of questions designed to help you explore your responses to feedback and criticism in three key areas: **cognitive reactions, emotional reactions, and behavioural reactions.**

Your response to these questions are useful at shining a light on how criticism affects you. It may even reveal patterns that might not have always been obvious. Although, I have to say, I'm not a psychologist or researcher. While I've taken great effort to make the self-assessment as relevant and bias-proof as possible, it should be used with the same sense of caution comes with doing any behavioural quiz from someone you don't know. Nevertheless, the results can help you to start taking more control of your reactions to criticism, and learn to manage it productively—even more resiliently.

## COGNITIVE REACTIONS: THOUGHTS ABOUT FEEDBACK

How do you interpret and mentally process feedback?

·   I often feel that criticism I receive is unfair.
·   When criticised, I feel that people don't understand my intentions.
·   When criticised, I feel it reflects poorly on my abilities or character.
·   I find myself replaying criticism over and over again in my mind.
·   I frequently feel that people overlook my strengths when they point out my mistakes.

Is feedback and criticism helpful or do you take it to heart? Generally, the more accurate the statements above, the more likely you are to view feedback as potentially threatening.

## EMOTIONAL REACTIONS:
## FEELINGS ABOUT FEEDBACK

What kind of emotional response does feedback stir in you?

- I feel resentment or irritation toward the person providing criticism.
- I often question the motives of people who give me feedback, wondering if it's coming from a genuine place.
- If I receive criticism, I'm less likely to continue with a task.
- I feel embarrassed after receiving negative feedback.
- I feel ashamed after receiving negative feedback.

Be it hurt, defensive, motivated or discouraged, pay attention to how criticism makes you feel. Does it motivate you to keep going or not? Your emotional reaction will determine how much you'll interact with feedback and how useful it will be over time. It will also help you know when you're likely to feel defensive or lack the confidence to seek it out in the first place.

## BEHAVIOURAL REACTIONS: RESPONSES TO FEEDBACK

What actions do you take in response to feedback and criticism? Do you change approach, avoid situations, or seek out more of it?

- I avoid environments or people where I might be criticised.
- I often explain myself or provide extra context when I receive negative feedback.
- I change my work or behaviour after receiving criticism to avoid future negative feedback.
- If I believe feedback is inaccurate or unfair, I will let the person know.
- I end up in arguments with the person providing criticism or feedback.

How does feedback affect your behaviour: Do you seek it or avoid it? What happens when you come into contact with it? If you're shying away from criticism or censoring yourself, taking baby steps toward changing the perception of feedback—from something hostile to something useful—can make all the difference.

As a general rule, the more the statements about your cognitive, emotional, and behavioural reactions ring true, the more likely it is that you're reacting to criticism in a way that doesn't help you—even avoiding situations where it might happen. But criticism isn't radioactive. The more comfortable you become with criticism, the easier you'll find it to embrace new ideas and knowledge. However, if the goal is to limit your exposure to criticism, it's going to be at the expense of testing and exploring new ideas and knowledge.

I have a theory that the tendency to hesitate and self-censor is because we think the price we'll pay for sharing something vague, half-baked, or poorly-received is greater than the benefit of the feedback and data we'll get in return. I'd even go so far as to say that reluctance is a symptom of a belief that if what we say is wrong or imperfect, we won't recover from it. In the end, even unconsciously, we end up guarded and secretive, hiding what's messy or uncertain because the criticism could turn out to be a liability.

# THE RIGHT KIND OF VULNERABILITY

Vulnerability is vital to creativity and divergent thinking, but not all vulnerabilities are the same. It's important to know the difference between when it helps and when it hinders. *Negative Vulnerability* comes from a place of fear; when we're so afraid of being judged that we don't want to hear criticism at all, and keep our ideas to ourselves, feeling too vulnerable to consider sharing. *Positive Vulnerability* is about allowing ourselves to be seen; welcoming criticism and other people's feedback as valuable data—not a threat to your value or self-esteem.

As we've explored, our sensitivity to criticism shapes how we approach risks, share ideas, and respond to setbacks. Reflecting on how we think, act, and behave is a first step towards building a more resilient, open mindset. But awareness alone isn't enough—we need to shift how we engage with feedback and vulnerability in our daily lives. This brings us to the next crucial step: building psychological safety through gradual exposure. By gradually facing discomfort in small, controlled steps, it's much easier to build a better foundation for taking risks with confidence and using criticism as a tool for growth.

# GRADUAL EXPOSURE

If vulnerability is such a critical ingredient to creativity, and you're either avoidant or highly sensitive to it, then the next step is to work on making it more of a part of your routine. We don't want to shy away from it, nor do we want to run head first into it unprepared. We want to find small, incremental ways to seek it out and interact with it more often over time, becoming more comfortable as we go.

Think of it as another muscle to exercise, like doing strength training at home or at a gym. If your exposure to feedback is consistent and controlled, you'll be in a much better place to build up strength and resistance—to use it to your advantage. Equally, if you don't put in the reps, your technique will suffer. It will be more difficult to maintain or improve. Eventually, those muscles will atrophy.

Like any new experience or routine, it's easy to put off those necessary first steps. We often worry that it's going to be more awkward and painful than it actually turns out to be. In your case, every piece of feedback could be an invaluable insight, every critique a breakthrough in your thinking or a strengthening of resolve—*shaping* and *perfecting* your ideas without knocking your self-esteem.

*Gradual Exposure* is a simple and powerful way of slowly facing things we fear or avoid and reducing their effect on us. The goal is to have fewer unhelpful reactions to criticism by becoming more comfortable with it one step at a time. Only then is it possible to use feedback as a tool for growth; turning criticism from something we dread into something that sharpens our ideas. With each step, you're not just building resilience, you're actively changing your relationship with vulnerability.

I want to reinforce something important: Vulnerability is not about exposing yourself to unnecessary risk or criticism. It's about recognising that growth and creativity often requires a step into the unknown. An openness to feedback and a willingness to fail and learn. Understanding our sensitivity to criticism, distinguishing between positive and negative vulnerability, and gradually exposing ourselves to constructive feedback, we can create an environment—both internally and externally—that encourages creativity. The goal isn't to become impervious to criticism. It's to develop the resilience and openness that allow you to use feedback as useful tool and to see uncertainty as an opportunity for something new.

As you navigate your own journey, positive vulnerability is a strength, not a weakness. It's when you're willing to be wrong that you'll often find your most brilliant ideas and your greatest potential for original thinking.

**Level One**

If you are: New to feedback or nervous about criticism.

**Level Two**

If you are: Comfortable with friendly feedback.

**Level Three**

If you are: Ready to push your comfort zone.

**Level Four**

If you are: Looking to increase confidence in sharing.

**Level Five**

If you are: Seeking diverse perspectives and visibility.

Then try: Sharing a rough idea with a close friend or mentor.

Start with someone you trust to give gentle, constructive feedback. This low-risk environment helps you focus on the feedback itself, rather than on the judgement.

Then try: Present to a small group of friends or colleagues.

Move to a slightly larger circle where feedback may be more varied. This helps you gain perspective from people who don't share your exact viewpoint.

Then try: Seek feedback from someone outside your usual circle.

Step outside your "safe zone" by sharing with someone unfamiliar. This will bring fresh perspectives and a more objective lens on your ideas.

Then try: Present to a larger audience or forum.

At this level, you're developing a resilience to critique. Present to a professional or mixed audiences, where feedback will be honest but potentially more critical.

Then try: Publish your idea or share in public forums.

Putting your ideas out in public increases exposure but also amplifies learning. Embrace this final step as an opportunity to iterate and refine through feedback.

# 3

From Caution to Control

# CONS
# EQUE
# NCES

# HARDWIRED FOR THE WORST

The doors close behind me with a whoosh and a hiss, and that's when it started. First it's my heart. It beats faster and faster. Surely everyone can hear it?! My face is hot. I must be glowing red. My feet feel glued to the floor. I'm sweating. I can't move. Am I breathing? Oh god. I need to *get out*.

This was my daily nightmare on the London Underground for years. Born and raised in Australia, I never thought about physical space as a finite resource, even in big cities like Sydney or Melbourne. Yet, after moving to London in 2015, I wasn't just figuring out a new chapter in life, I was also introduced to the twice-daily torture of squeezing myself into a metal tube some 25 metres underground just to get to work.

The experience was always the same. I'd enter the station, pass through the ticket barrier, and descend into a subterranean hellscape that somehow maintained an average temperature twice that of the world above*. Making my way towards the train, I would reassure myself that it's completely safe to travel underground. Millions of people do it everyday. But as more and more fellow commuters squeezed their way onto the platform, I would feel the apprehension building. Like the tension of waiting for a jump scare in a horror film. I knew something was about to happen. I just didn't know exactly when.

* In 2017, the BBC ran a story of temperatures on London's Central Line exceeding the legal limit for transporting livestock. It's not only temperature: Passengers are also crammed into far less space than cattle are legally allowed.

As I stood in the crowd, the train would burst from its dark tunnel at the end of the platform, and everyone would jostle towards the doors as it came to a full stop. I'd always hang back slightly. My theory being: If you're last on the train, you're closer to the doors and therefore safer (or less confined) than if you were sandwiched between fellow passengers in the aisle, unable to get out in an emergency.

As the doors closed and the train left the station, my chest began to tighten. The air turned solid—or so it seemed. Trying to fill my lungs, it felt like breathing through a straw. With every second passing, the carriage walls would get closer and closer. My grip on the handrail would get tighter and tighter. That handrail felt like my only link to what was real. My palms wet with nervous sweat, a flood of disastrous scenarios would hit me. How many people suffocate to death on the underground each year? How many trains get stuck in these dark tunnels forever? Time slowed. The minutes between stations moved at a glacial pace. Closing my eyes and turning up the volume on my headphones only intensified the feeling of being trapped. If I wasn't hyper-aware, I thought, then I wasn't in control.

This was my personal hell for over a year: Claustrophobia on the London Underground. Millions of people travel on the underground every day without a second thought. But for me, every journey was a fight or flight situation. Until finally one day, after lasting only one stop, elbowing my way to the carriage doors and walking for over an hour in the pouring rain, I knew I needed to do something.

So what did I do? I went to some experts. And not just

because of my hellish rides on the underground—the same fear had started to present itself in other places: Cars, planes, elevators, and even crowded supermarkets became a problem. I wasn't about to let this fear rule my life in a city where the underground is like a second home. So, I shopped around—speaking to all kinds of doctors and specialists. I was on a mission to understand what was going on in my brain and how to fix it, or at least live with it.

In a session with one consulting psychotherapist, Catherine, she mentioned how parts of our brain don't know the difference between a real threat and an imagined one. The *amygdala* is a tiny, peanut-sized part of the brain buried deep in the temporal lobe is the fear centre of our 'lizard brain'. It's the primitive part of grey matter that's been keeping us alive since we were dodging sabertooth tigers.

When the amygdala senses danger, real or imagined, it sets off a cascade of automated responses in your body. It floods your system with stress hormones like cortisol and adrenaline. Your heart rate skyrockets, your breathing quickens, your muscles tense up. It's the fight-or-flight response, and it's happening before the rational part of your brain has the chance to weigh in. To this prehistoric part of my brain, a crowded Tube carriage might as well have been the jaws of a predator. It was working on autopilot, following a script written thousands of years ago. Learning about this didn't magically cure my claustrophobia, but it gave me something to investigate more deeply. I wasn't just some neurotic mess. There was a biological reason behind why I felt like I was going to die.

Everyone has an amygdala that can be tricked into hyperdrive in different situations. I might have experienced something bad in a crowded environment and, thus, any crowded environment would trigger a coded response from long ago. I might even just have seen a movie about something that made me think crowded places were dangerous and imagined some worst-case scenarios. Basically, something, whatever it might have been, set my amygdala working overtime. Biologically and evolutionary speaking, we're wired to catastrophise so we're ready to dodge threats to our safety and survival.

Do you have any irrational fears? For some people, it might be the paralysis before hitting send on an important email: The seemingly small worry that there's a typo or that the email will be misread sends their amygdala into overdrive and they react as if they were being served up as dinner to predators. Or it could be their hesitation to speak up in a meeting, as they are scared of looking stupid. These fears, big and small, all stem from the hardwired aversion to negative consequences because our brain believes any negative consequence to be potentially fatal.

This tendency to catastrophise was useful when we were avoiding becoming lunch for prehistoric predators. But in our modern world, it's often an overreaction; a protective mechanism in overdrive. It's the voice in your head saying "what if" before you've even had a chance to consider "why not."

**While this instinct to expect the worst kept our ancestors alive, it's now more likely to hold us back. It dampens our potential for taking risks, trying new things,**

**or expressing ourselves fully. Our lizard brain, in its attempt to keep us safe, is inadvertently suffocating our capacity for developing new and divergent ideas.**

But here's the good news: Understanding this biological process is the first step in reclaiming control. Once you know that your amygdala is just doing its job—albeit a bit too enthusiastically—you can start to work with it, rather than against it. You can learn to recognise when it's overreacting and use different tools to calm it down. We will explore two of those tools in this chapter.

In the meantime, the next time you feel that familiar surge of panic, whether it's on the Tube or before a big presentation, remember: It's just your lizard brain trying to keep you safe. Acknowledge it, thank it for its concern, and then decide if that concern is actually warranted in the current situation. (It usually isn't.)

Anything new comes with uncertainty, forcing the brain to predict outcomes, often the most negative. But acting on those predictions and avoiding risks entirely comes with a tax on originality. Or worse, turns the exploration of something new into anxiety. Every great idea, every breakthrough, stems not simply from accepting mistakes as a part of the process, but learning to manage and minimise the scope of them. Only when we learn to use our innate instinct to avoid consequences as a tool, and begin to see them as necessary steps for original thinking do we liberate creativity.

# THE MYTH OF RATIONALITY

Avoiding *consequences* seems rational, but the flaw in this assumption is that we're rational by default. In 2005, on my first day of classes at university, I sat in a large auditorium for Microeconomics 101. The lecturer walked in, introduced himself, and then faced the 200 or so students in the room.

"Welcome to Microeconomics 101," he said.

No one said anything.

"Can anyone tell me what Microeconomics is?" he asked.

Again, no one said anything. Then after about 20 seconds...

"Yes?" he said, pointing in my direction.

I didn't know then, but someone had raised their hand behind me. I have to be honest, I was already nervous. Admitting that I didn't know the answer, and didn't even have the confidence to wing it, would have been too much for Day 1 of university. While my brain switched from logical thought to white noise, the person behind me spoke up.

"It's the study of people buying things," he said.

"Not exactly," said the lecturer.

He then scanned the auditorium to choose one of the other raised hands, but everyone had put them down. Ah, welcome to the cowards club everyone, I thought. You are my people.

The lecturer then explained that in Economics, we'd be studying the basic concepts about how individuals make decisions. But that wasn't everything. We'd also explore how resources are allocated, not just people's money to buy things, but how businesses and governments deploy them. We'd look at different situations that shape the supply and demand of goods, and how various interventions can move people and whole economies in the right direction. But there was something we should know before we started.

"For hundreds of years, the field of economics has based a lot of its modelling and theory on the idea of the perfectly rational person." He explained, "But that's wrong."

The perfectly 'rational' human being, or *Homo Economicus*' as it's known, is a convenient invention. The idea is that in any scenario, a person will make the most efficient use of their time, money, and energy to get as much satisfaction and happiness as possible. Almost all economic theory since the 19th century is based on the notion that people will make 'rational' decisions that maximise their own interests. It still underpins a lot of how society and economies are designed today. But there's a flaw.

Humans are a far cry from perfectly rational entities. Most social scientists, psychologists, and pioneers of behavioural economics believe that Homo Economicus should be debunked. People make decisions for a lot of reasons. These are sometimes visible and straightforward, such as choosing to buy one product over another because it's half the price. Other times they're not so clear or logical, like doubling down on a losing streak. Nobel Prize winners Daniel Kahneman and Amos Tversky say that human beings think and make decisions in two different ways, which they call System 1 and System 2 thinking.

*System 1* is how we make quick and intuitive decisions, often automatically. Like swerving your car to avoid a collision. *System 2* is more deliberate and logical. It's when we take our time and consider options. Like weighing up the pros and cons of a job offer in a new city. Truthbetold, it's not as simple as that. The line between rational and irrational thinking is more blurred than we like to admit. We're swimming in a sea of subtle cues, gut feelings, and deeply ingrained habits—often unaware how much our decisions are influenced by them. In one study, behavioural economist Dan Ariely asked participants to write down the last two digits of their social security number before bidding on items in an auction. Incredibly, those with higher numbers at the end of their social security number consistently bid higher amounts than those with lower numbers. Supposedly rational minds were being swayed by completely irrelevant information, which is a worry when a lot of the time we're unaware of it. Perhaps the idea of 'clearing our mind' before making a decision isn't a bad idea after all.

A fundamental barrier to creativity and innovation is how dependent we can become on flawed rationality. When starting to create or execute on new ideas, we tend to switch back and forth between our automatic and intuitive System 1 thinking and the more deliberate and analytical System 2. But unlike Homo Economicus, much of our decision making is muddled with subconscious biases and imperfect information. Even when trying to think rationally, these can cloud our thinking or cause us to miss key aspects—both positive and negative—of the creative process. This not only prevents the full realisation of new ideas but also acts as a blocker to navigating the complexities of bringing something novel into existence.

## CURSED WITH BIAS

The conversation around bias is one that's started to gain real momentum. While it's great that this conversation is happening, it does mean that the term bias can become a little loaded. In the context of this book, I want to be clear about the biases I'm referring to. They are the mental shortcuts we've inherited to work through everyday decisions—ways that early human beings made quick decisions when the environment was uncertain, making the best use of scarce cognitive resources.

You and I are still running on a lot of that same cognitive programming today. When we face any decision, our minds rarely start with a blank slate. Instead, it quickly draws on hard coding in our evolution, personality traits, information we know, and past experiences to predict what to expect. Psychological researchers Professor Patric Bach and Dr. Kim Schenke say that as we gather more details about any situation or decision, our brains use new information to test our initial hunches. Sometimes, our early predictions are right, making us more confident in our judgement. Other times, we're wrong, forcing us to revise our thinking. As a general rule, this process helps us navigate the world efficiently. But it also shows our decisions can be distorted. Understanding this, even only to the level of being aware of it, help as a reminder of how skewed our perspective can be. There are three biases that I want us to consider in the context of how we perceive, plan for, and react to consequences: Loss Aversion, Availability Bias, and Negativity Bias.

Understanding these biases can help you catch them before they overly influence your decisions. While they never disappear entirely, even a little awareness helps you to frame questions more effectively, consider a broader range of options, and ultimately think more objectively. By taking these steps, you can make more balanced and informed choices when facing risks.

## LOSS AVERSION BIAS

You are more likely to hold on to $100 you already have rather than risk it on a 50/50 bet to win $200. **We prefer to avoid losses rather than obtain equal gains. Put simply, we suffer more intensely at losing something than we enjoy at gaining something of the same worth.**

## AVAILABILITY BIAS

If you hear a news story about a plane crash, your perception of the danger of flying is temporarily elevated, even though statistically flying is safer than most forms of travel. **We overestimate the frequency and presence of things that are 'available' in our memory, either because they occurred recently or in an emotionally charged way.**

## NEGATIVITY BIAS

After giving a presentation to five people, you get four compliments and one criticism. You then spend more time fixating on that one negative comment than the four positive ones. **We pay more attention to negative experiences and information than positive ones. It's a trait that taught early human beings how to adapt and survive.**

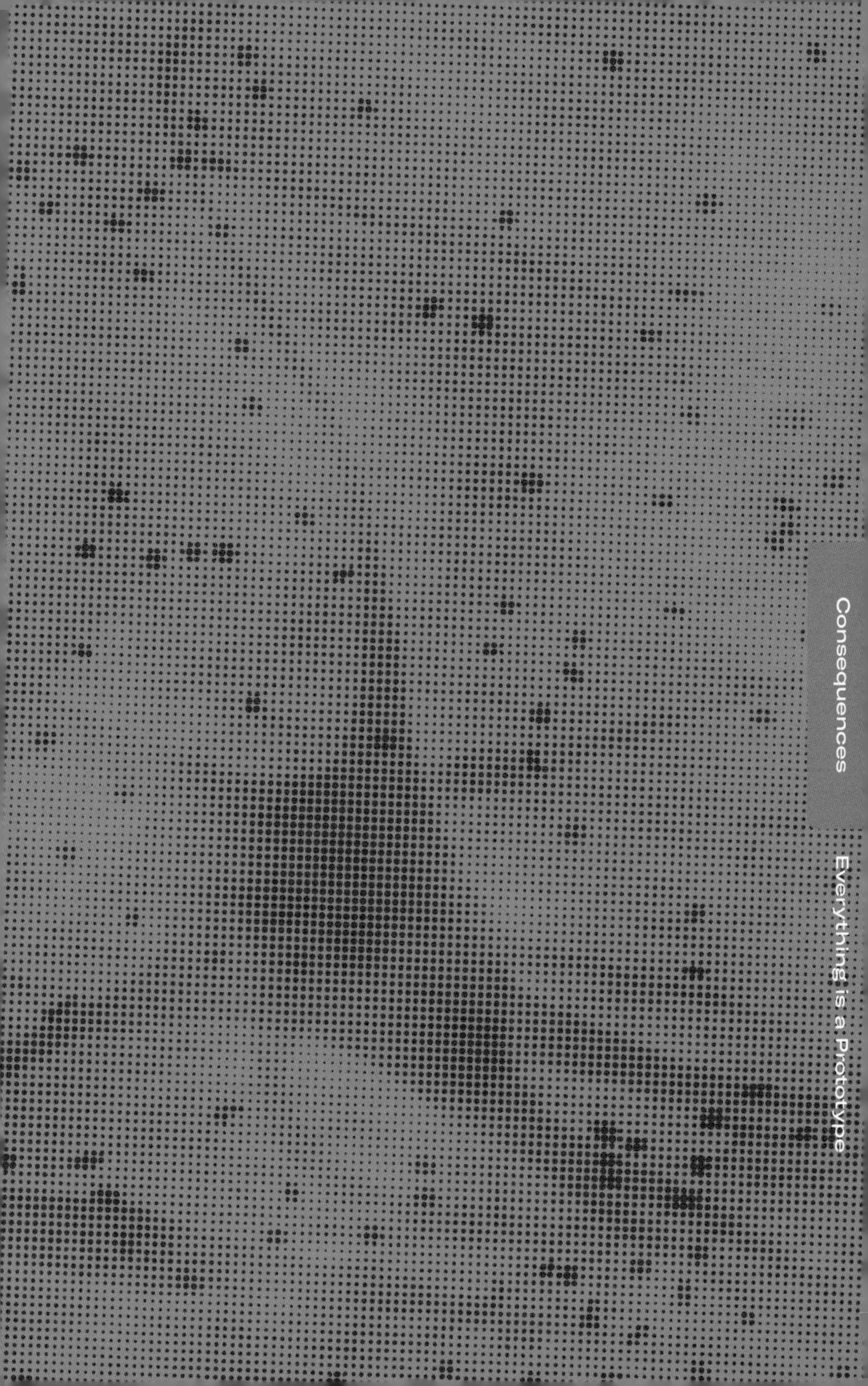

# THE SPECTRUM
# OF SEVERITY

By default, we aren't driven to maximise happiness at any cost. Instead, we're driven to minimise the consequences of being wrong. Self-preservation becomes the only goal. We're constantly working to save face by avoiding making mistakes that would make us look bad, or in some other way hurt us. Our reptilian brain is hardwired to avoid consequences because it equates them to pain, isolation, or even death. But we're no longer living in prehistoric times. Consequences, as far as those that come with testing out the validity of an idea, rarely equal anything severe. And while it can come with other negative consequences, there are ways to lessen them. In short, the way we provoke and test and learn can in itself minimise risk without taxing the potential of what we're trying to achieve.

To help understand and control your response to potential consequences, it is useful to think of them on a spectrum of severity. It's not the perfect cure for being overly risk averse, but it does help frame your thinking. It makes it possible to be more nuanced when considering and making decisions that have risks, instead of avoiding them altogether (or rushing in without a care in the world, just in case your amygdala is of the lazy variety, because, while we haven't spoken about it thus far, there are people who rush in where others fear to tread). By thinking of consequences on a spectrum with the goal of moving from Severe to Mild, our actions can become more thoughtful than bets to be won or lost. It helps us divide ideas and decisions into smaller pieces, reducing the odds of the most severe consequences if things do go wrong.

## SEVERE CONSEQUENCES

**A loss there's no coming back from.** A head first collision with the worst outcome. Whether it's the loss of livelihood or even lives, the consequences of a total failure are absolute—like gambling everything you own on a bet: If you lose, you lose everything.

## ACUTE CONSEQUENCES

**A bad setback with a possibility of recovery.** Picture a house where the roof is peeled away in a storm. The house is still intact. It doesn't have to be rebuilt from the ground up. It's not a minor setback but it's not a disaster. These kinds of larger, acute, failures need a lot of effort and attention to fix and, more often than not, they force you to completely pause everything else until they're resolved.

## MILD CONSEQUENCES

**A speed bump that teaches you more than it taxes.** This kind of consequence could be reversible or isolated; meaning that even when they do come with a cost of any kind, they're minor or easily managed. However, don't be mistaken; even a mild failure is a powerful lesson, so much that it's important to make sure you're not avoiding them at the cost of failing to learn and iterate.

## BALANCING PRESSURE, BIAS, AND BETTER DECISIONS

Imagine you're balancing on a thin wire that's strung between two high-rise buildings. If you're too relaxed, you'll probably lose focus and fall. If you're riddled with fear, your muscles will tense up, become rigid and unstable, and you'll also fall. Both of these scenarios end in the most severe of consequences. However, there can be a useful middleground that keeps you alert and cautious but also moving forward.

A popular psychology concept known as Yerkes-Dodson Law suggests that the right amount of *pressure* leads to better performance. For example, nerves before a big exam helps with memory and recall, or butterflies before stepping on stage to give a talk helps you stay focussed on your key message. The theory is that a bit of pressure actually puts us in a better state, but only up to a certain point. Too much stress, they say, has the opposite effect, bringing your performance to a nosedive.

I should emphasise that Yerkes-Dodson Law isn't a scientific fact. In fact, it has been called out by researchers as something not to be used empirically. Dr. Martin Corbett from the University of Leicester warned of "the publication of long-discredited models of stress and performance" and the popularity of certain people and businesses to use the 'law' as permission to ramp up stress and anxiety to increase productivity.

In our context, we don't want to add stress or risks, we're trying to minimise it. We want to understand potential consequences and make plans to work around them. But we must remember we'll never remove it entirely and that a little bit of stress isn't necessarily a bad thing. It could even be useful.

By now you might be thinking, 'Great, so my brain is pessimistic, risk averse and so riddled with bias that I can't even trust my own thinking?' Well, it might not be good news, but being aware of what's going on, it can be used more wisely. You can take the power back. Just like I learned to manage claustrophobia on the London Underground by understanding what's happening in my brain, you can use the knowledge of these biases to your advantage.

You aren't going to ignore your biases or pretend they don't exist. That would be like trying to open a door while ignoring it's locked. And while the two methods we'll look at won't 'cure' the risk of consequences entirely, they can teach us how to work with them, reduce them overall, and redirect our natural talent for predicting the worst outcomes by taking that pessimistic streak and turning it into something useful. The goal of these two methods is to *prepare* you for possibilities that can stem from your decisions, and minimise or avoid the worst of consequences by *pre – empting* the causes that lead to them.

# PRE-EMPTING

The best preparation for consequences is to plan for them. While we can't predict every possible outcome, *Pre Mortems* and *Consequence Mapping* are powerful tools for anticipating the worst and doing our best to avoid it, or at least minimise it.

Rather than being reactive in the moment, these simple frameworks help us to get more intentional and start to plan how we might avoid the most severe of consequences by taking steps to pre-empt them. Like the human body, a post-mortem might help to explain why someone died, but it can't bring them back after the worst has happened. The best thing to know is what could be done to prevent the worst in the first place.

# PRE-MORTEM

# PRE-MORTEM

**How could this all go terribly wrong?
And what can be done to prevent it?**

If our brains are predisposed to focus on the negative, a Pre-Mortem turns the inner pessimist into something useful. It's a way of flipping the question, 'what's the worst that could happen?' and turning it into a *time machine* that enables you to reflect upon how a decision, idea, or problem could go wrong, and plan ways to prevent it from being a total failure... perhaps even turning it into a raging success.

Instead of hoping for the best and then finding yourself unprepared when it doesn't happen, you're going to work backwards from a future where the worst has happened. Like knowing what you'll do if the airline loses your luggage on the way to a wedding, or who you'll turn to if a tradesperson disappears during a renovation. But it's not just about imagining something bad and having a pre-canned action. It's about preventing the worst from happening in the first place.

One particularly interesting example is when a San Diego health centre used the Pre-Mortem on a COVID-19 testing program before it was implemented. Patients and providers were asked to imagine that the testing strategy had failed and work backwards to identify possible reasons. The results revealed several important insights: Potential barriers to the testing strategy working at all; a list of issues that could be addressed before it was rolled out; and a head start on solving them. This gave them a chance to pre-empt, avoid, and resolve the most visible problems before they happened.

# INSTRUCTIONS

The *Pre-Mortem* is a powerful technique because it gives you a preview of the difficulties that may occur before they do. It's a cheat code for any decision or creative process. It takes advantage of that negativity bias we talked about earlier, using the pessimism and caution that your brain is naturally wired to focus on.

Keep in mind that the goal is not to scare you into not pursuing any new idea or venture at all. The goal is to prepare for the worst, pre-empt what you can, while hoping for the best. When you plan for the worst and how to prevent or minimise it, you are becoming more free to take bigger risks, mindfully, and more carefully. After all, once you've imagined the worst case scenario, everything else looks a little less scary.

## 1

### Imagine the Worst

Picture your idea, dream, or project failing spectacularly in the future. Describe the failure as if it's happening today—what went wrong, and how bad is it?

## 2

### Find the Blame

List every possible reason for the failure. Did it solve the wrong problem? Did someone else do it better? Was time, money, or patience the issue? No cause is too big or small—write them all down.

**3**

## Start Digging

Examine each reason and ask: Why did this happen? Was it naivety, overconfidence, missing information, or poor timing? Let your inner critic explore every angle.

**4**

## Plan a Defence

For every potential cause of failure, think about what could have been done differently. What decisions, actions, or information might have prevented disaster?

**5**

## Decide on First Steps

Turn insights into actions. What can you start doing now to avoid these failures? Break big decisions into smaller ones, seek missing information, or reduce severe risks into manageable ones.

# CONSEQUENCE MAPPING

# CONSEQUENCE MAPPING

**How can I navigate the best and worst-case scenarios if they do happen?**

What are the potential outcomes of starting to go to the gym three times per week? Losing weight, better mental health, a boost in confidence could be some. Equally, it's possible that the outcome could be a physical injury, or less free time to do other things you enjoy. While this is a simplistic example, it's the same approach to any action; whether you've got a complex decision or challenge in front of you, you're pursuing an idea or change that's likely to take a long time, or involve lots of variables. What you want to understand are the consequences of your *choices*. Ideally before you make irreversible ones.

Where a Pre-Mortem imagines the *worst* possible future outcome and works its way back through all the potential reasons it happened, Consequence Mapping is like a GPS for exploring different scenarios that stem from actions and decisions before you make them. A Pre-Mortem gets you ready to prevent a total failure, while Consequence Mapping lets you navigate multiple scenarios in the *future*. Using them both can be a powerful approach to foreseeing (and ideally avoiding) the most severe of consequences.

Here's how *Consequence Mapping* works: Instead of just thinking you will succeed or fail, you're going to create a map of potential outcomes stemming from the original action, both good and bad. It's like playing a game of chess several moves ahead of your opponent, giving you a sense of possible directions the game can go. Now, instinctively you avoid disaster, but it's more than that, it's about understanding the entire spectrum of potential outcomes. Let's now dive into how we make a Consequence Map and get started finding our way through the choppy waters of decision making.

*3*

**Assess the Outcomes**

**Define the Decision or Action**

*1*

*2*

**Identify Potential Outcomes**

What's the specific decision or action you want to take? Example: Adopting a dog from a local shelter.

Are these outcomes good, bad, or neutral? Which do you want, which would you prefer to avoid, and which don't bother you? Example: Want: Loyal companionship. Avoid: Vet bills. Neutral: Daily routine changes.

What are all the possible outcomes of this decision? Example: Gaining a companion, increased exercise, unexpected vet bills, changes to routine, etc.

## 5

### Evaluate Risks and Likelihood

What are the risks if your assumptions are wrong? How likely are the different outcomes and their consequences to happen? Example: Risk: Dog may have behavioral issues. Likelihood: Medium.

## 4

### Understand Assumptions

What assumptions are you making about why these outcomes will occur? Are these assumptions within your control? Example: Assumption: The dog will be active and encourage exercise. Reality: The dog's age, breed, or health might not align with this assumption.

## 6

### Plan Actions

How can you encourage desirable outcomes and minimise undesirable ones? What actions or information will help? Example: Action: Research breeds, meet the dog multiple times before adopting, and budget for unforeseen vet expenses.

# THERE WILL BE BLINDSPOTS

The problem with not knowing what you don't know is that you don't know that you don't know it. (Stay with me.) That's an area where you're going to have to accept a degree of uncertainty, but there's also a way to minimise the severity of it, if things do go wrong.

People sometimes make the assumption that a Pre-Mortem will unearth *everything* that can possibly happen, good or bad. None of these methods can predict the future. They're crutches for becoming comfortable with ambiguity, as opposed to freezing (and not acting on ideas) because of it.

Don't reprimand yourself for things you can't see or predict. Rather, appreciate the opportunity to wrestle as many potential events as you can. By considering them, you're already expanding the surface area for logical and critical thinking, opening up possibilities that you might otherwise not have considered.

Consequences may feel like looming *threats*, but when they're preempted and minimised, you can build the right guardrails around ideas and decisions and still make good progress. By avoiding the worst consequences, it's possible to shift focus from total failure to embracing the iterative nature of testing and learning as you go. Not all consequences are catastrophic; in fact, most fall on a spectrum, with many of them offering insights to make ideas and decisions even stronger. Understanding this helps us make smarter, more intentional decisions about which risks are worth taking.

Ingenuity doesn't happen when you avoid risks. The truth is, staying safe often means staying still. Breakthroughs come from stepping into uncertainty with purpose and intention. Instead of being paralysed by the worst-case scenario, we can learn to manage consequences, making room for exploration and discovery. By breaking challenges into smaller, more manageable parts, it's possible to create space for risks to become valuable hacks for learning and growth.

This is a book primarily about ideas and creativity— how to approach things more experimentally while taking precautions to avoid irreversible mistakes. It's about finding ways to think and work boldly, without risking everything in the process. And while creativity and innovation are at its heart, the principles here apply to any area where you're navigating new territory, whether that's launching a project, starting a career, or developing a personal goal.

Imagine a new venture you're considering, perhaps a job change or a side project. What's the best possible outcome? What are you assuming would make that outcome likely? And on the flip side, what would a setback look like, and what would lead to that? Identifying these possibilities helps you spot where you can plan and prepare, applying the tools in this book to clarify your vision and improve your decision-making. In doing so, you build confidence to pursue what excites you while mitigating the risks of blind spots or untested assumptions.

At its core, the goal is to become more creatively *resilient*. By examining the full spectrum of outcomes, we don't just improve our ideas; we become more realistic in how we execute them. This approach turns dreams into workable plans and helps avoid the kind of oversights that stall progress, bringing us closer to sustainable success in whatever we choose to pursue.

As we move into the next section of the book, it's important to remember that the decision to engage with consequences—when controlled and intentional—is the foundation of all good prototyping and experimentation. We don't want reckless abandon; we want to find ways to navigate the unknown safely, gathering data and refining our ideas. Every step of the experimental phase reduces the weight of consequences, teaches us lessons, and turns being wrong into a shortcut for genuine breakthroughs. In the next chapter, you'll discover how experimentation allows us to harness feedback, iterate quickly, and make *better mistakes*.

# 4

You Can't Predict, But You Can Provoke

# EXPER
# IMENT
# ATION

# EXPERIMENTATION

**Wisdom isn't a byproduct of unwavering belief in a single idea; it's the result of nurturing many, often competing, ideas at the same time.**

*The Bill Murray* is a small but influential comedy club tucked away in an affluent back street of Islington. It has all the hallmarks of a classic comedy venue: a dimly lit theatre, low ceilings, rehearsal spaces, a well-stocked bar, and a rotating cast of comedians performing every night. On the wall outside, against a backdrop of dark paint and blacked-out windows, is a tribute to some of the world's funniest people: Richard Pryor, Whoopi Goldberg, Billy Connolly, and of course, flanking the entrance, an 8ft tall picture of Bill Murray himself. If you've enjoyed a British standup comedian in the last ten years, there's a chance that what you laughed at was first tested in front of an audience.

What sets it apart from other venues is that it's not just a place to perform—it's a place to *experiment* and develop new material. Known for its 'work-in-progress' shows, the club is something like a laboratory where comedians test and iterate on new material with a live audience, gauging what lands and what doesn't in *real time.* Every stand-up routine, no matter how polished, starts as a rough draft. Even comedy legends like Jerry Seinfeld try out early ideas in order to refine their sets long before they hit the big stages. They tweak, rearrange, and discard bits through countless hours of iteration—all in search of a tighter punchline, a sharper setup, or the perfect structure and delivery. The process is messy, uncomfortable, and sometimes painful. But it's the only way to turn what the American author Anne Lamott calles a 'shitty first draft' of an idea into a solid routine.

The beauty of comedy lies in its honesty. There's no sugarcoating when a joke falls flat. Audience feedback are immediate, unforgiving, and transparent. If a joke is funny, people will laugh. If it isn't funny, they won't. Their unfiltered reactions cut straight to the truth: Did it work or did it fail? How well received was it? Did it have everyone in stitches, or was it a mixed bag of reactions? And yet, the best comics know that even the jokes that bomb one night might still have potential. A small tweak in the setup, a change in timing, or a fresh perspective can transform it from a dud to a crowd-pleaser.

This relentless pursuit of refinement is the essence of experimentation: a willingness to confront failure, learn from it, and then come back again with something better. The lesson: Progress doesn't come from playing it safe—it comes from constant trial, error, and iteration. And it happens one experiment at a time.

# NEVER-ENDING "WORK IN PROGRESS"

"*Comedy is a brutal art form,*" says comedian Fin Taylor. "The audience decides everything." Unlike other creative pursuits, where ideas can be shaped in solitude, comedy is tested and refined, with the audience serving as the judge and jury. Their reactions—laughter, silence, or even rejection—are immediate, unfiltered, and objective.

Before stepping on stage for a show, Taylor presses record on his phone and places it in his back pocket. This small act is part of a larger process of dissecting his standup, replaying every moment to answer the essential questions: Was it funny? Was the delivery right? Is this line better than that line? Each recording becomes a tool for refining the raw material of his jokes, transforming them from rough drafts on paper into polished lines performed live.

Work-in-progress shows, like those at *The Bill Murray*, provide the perfect environment for this iterative approach. Taylor describes them as "a space to Indiana Jones my way through the new stuff." By starting with tried-and-true material, he builds trust with the audience before leading them into uncharted territory. "Some gigs are for them, and some gigs are for you," he says. These shows are undeniably for the comedian—a chance to test ideas, embrace failure, and discover what works.

The process is messy, but it's how standup comedy comes to life. A joke that falls flat one night might be reworked into a crowd-pleaser through a small tweak in timing or tone. As Taylor explains, "If they don't laugh, you know exactly what needs to change." The audience isn't just a passive observer; they're an integral part of the process, shaping each joke with their unvarnished reactions.

A comedy set might begin as a rough draft, but it's nurtured and perfected through constant *feedback*. Every laugh, pause, or silence provides a data point for Taylor's ongoing experiment. The result? A routine that feels seamless and spontaneous, built on countless iterations of trial and error. In comedy, there's no such thing as finished—only better.

## THE SCIENTIFIC METHOD AS A FRAMEWORK

We often hear that the secret to some of the world's greatest ideas and inventions are the result of *happy accidents*. It's a romantic notion that they're just sitting there, waiting for someone to find them. Take Alexander Fleming as an example. He may have discovered penicillin after returning from holiday and finding mould in a petri dish. However, it's not the full picture. He had set up trays of Staphylococci (a bacteria that leads to many nasty diseases) before he left for vacation. It was only by noticing the strange effect the mould had on the bacteria when he returned that led to the world's first antibiotic.

A mouldy coffee cup in a sink wouldn't have yielded the same results. Now, I'm not underestimating a certain degree of circumstance or good timing, but the reality is that Fleming had to create the right situation for a breakthrough to happen, even if he was unsure exactly what shape it might take.

Experimentation is the act of testing a hypothesis. Or to put it more simply, finding out what the effect of one thing has on another. It's about asking questions and observing results in controlled environments. Outside of science, it's a buzzword for business, especially the tech industry that I come from. Google once tested more than *40 shades of blue* for the colour of paid links they were launching in Gmail. Supposedly, they found through multiple rounds of testing the shade of blue that led to more clicks, and hence more advertising dollars. It was worth it in the end. One insider said, "given the scale of our business...we made an extra $200m a year in ad revenue."

This chapter isn't going to focus on business experiments, but rather the underlying idea that experimentation is a powerful tool for discovery and innovation in lots of places. Whether you're a scientist working in a lab, an artist experimenting with new techniques, or simply a human striving for ways to make the best of a routine—the benefit is universal.

We'll start with the basic principles: How to design good experiments, how to determine what we're testing, and how to observe and interpret the results. To illustrate, we'll dive into examples from different fields, and how experiments have made a difference. We'll look at how you can use experimentation as a way of testing ideas and understanding the world around you to solve new problems.

I'll also talk about the *Experimental Mindset* —one that is filled with curiosity, treats failure as a learning event, and keeps an open eye for the unexpected. This is important, not least because some of the greatest breakthroughs in history have stemmed from researchers being aware of results they had not intended to find—like Fleming's discovery of penicillin. He was curious and kept an eye out for the unexpected. Had he not, he'd just have tossed that mould in the bin, annoyed that things hadn't gone as planned. Instead, he got curious and decided to investigate.

At the end of this chapter, you'll have a grasp of how to start applying experimental thinking to your own life and work. If you're keen on innovating, solving problems or just plain-old wondering how things work, the principles of experimentation we'll explore can help you approach challenges more systematically and creatively.

## QUASI-EXPERIMENTS, NOT PURE EXPERIMENTS.

At its most fundamental, experimentation is a bridge between imagination and reality. It's not just a series of steps to follow for ideas to be explored and tested—it's also a mindset that embraces curiosity and adaptability to data and feedback. Great ideas are useless when they're hidden from the real world. They have to move from the theoretical and into the tangible. This is the only way you can explore, find evidence, and decide what to do next. So that idea for a book, a new business, roadtrip, design for a dress, getting married, having a child...you can get started by experimenting, finding evidence, and deciding what to do next. (When it comes to experimentation around having a child...we're not talking about getting someone pregnant, but rather learning what it's like looking after another life...a very small, loud, and nappy-filled life that later will learn to slam doors and mess up their bedroom).

The goal of this chapter is to help you test ideas by running *Quasi – Experiments*. They differ from pure scientific experiments in one critical way: they don't need perfect control or strictly isolated variables. They're tests done in the real world, where conditions are less controllable. Pure experiments need precision and rigour in well controlled settings, whereas quasi-experiments are about testing cheaply and quickly, knowing that some factors won't be predictable or accounted for.

A pure experiment might be done in a controlled lab where you're testing what one thing does to another. If you did this in a quasi-experiment you would test the same question in a more *natural* or *practical* setting and acknowledge that variables might overlap. For example, instead of testing how a dress design will look under particular lighting in a controlled studio, you would take it to a busy shop floor to see how people will react to it in the real world. Quasi experiments are scrappier but more adaptable. You can try things without the need for perfection—making feedback and your learning cycle a lot faster. Only then will you have a clue whether to run with something, change it, or ditch it entirely.

With experimentation of this kind, you turn your visions into reality in a thoughtful, incremental way, without the all-or-nothing ultimatum. In *Consequences*, we already discussed that there's no such thing as trying new or different without risk. But if you let assumptions go unchallenged and ideas go untested, you'll eventually face one of two outcomes: Potentially great ideas left on the shelf, never putting them out into the world, or investing time and effort into repairing, pivoting, or bailing far too late.

## BOILING THE OCEAN

You can't boil the ocean. At least that's what I remind people when facing new challenges. Whether you're trying to develop a new technology or unravel the mysteries of human cognition, breaking up big questions into bite-sized chunks is the shortcut to finding the answers, faster. Not to mention minimising the cost of getting it wrong. However, looking at the component parts of any question is only half the battle. You also need to know how to find the right data as feedback. That's where experiments come in. However, I use the word 'data' liberally here. I don't limit data to only the purely quantifiable, I'm also looking for the vague and sometimes unmeasurable—to understand the shades of grey that aren't as accessible as facts and numbers—in a way that helps an idea or question evolve and iterate, or be abandoned.

More often than not, the data you're looking for doesn't exist. Or conventional wisdom says it's difficult to find, so you don't seek it out. It's here that the power of experimentation really shines. With a little effort, we can generate new data by finding ways to test or bust our assumptions, and explore entirely uncharted territory of our knowledge. It's a way of directly and indirectly finding answers. Take dark matter research for example. Scientists know that an invisible "dark matter" makes up much of the universe, but what it is and how it behaves is still mysterious. Rather than throw in the towel, researchers have developed clever experiments to catch a glimpse of its indirect effects, such as gravity, to build a deeper understanding. That's all experimentation is: The search for data to help make the unknown a little clearer. And that's what we're looking for. Even if it's not the full picture.

When we design and run experiments, we typically trip over new questions, find answers we didn't expect, or discover that our initial assumptions were wrong. Rather than setbacks, these "failures" are chances to learn and even to refine our own understanding, if done correctly. Experimentation is not about verifying ideas we already know or suspect (so kiss your ego goodbye, because this isn't about trying to prove a point). It's about seeking evidence where there isn't any. At its core, it's about being okay with not knowing, and using that not knowing to drive your exploration. In the following pages we'll delve into experimentation and prototyping techniques, we'll use them to ask and answer questions, test hypotheses, and create new data (and discoveries). The more you do this, the more surface area you'll be creating to do new and different things.

1. **OBSERVE**

2. **HYPOTHESISE**

3. **PROTOTYPE**

4. **TEST**

# HOW TO EXPERIMENT

Experimentation is all about taking an idea and making it real. The approach I'm laying out here is simple but effective, rooted in research, and honed through plenty of trial and error. But this isn't about lab-perfect science; it's about rolling up your sleeves and taking practical, actionable steps to explore, test, and refine through data and feedback. There are four key phases:

1. Observe
2. Hypothesise
3. Prototype
4. Test

Each phase is unique and is designed to be used in order. The outputs of one stage are important building blocks for the next. And while there's always a certain amount of *fuzziness* at the edges, I don't suggest skipping or shortcutting your way through the process, hoping to get to the results more quickly. This isn't about taking shortcuts—it's about thoughtful and deliberate experimentation.

Every step of the process is designed to give you the information and insights you need for the one that follows. By embracing it in order, you'll be able to make confident decisions, adjust as needed, and ultimately arrive at a solution that's stronger and more refined. Let's dive in.

*(Phase 1)*

# OBSERVE

"It is through observing that we learn, develop knowledge, and in turn gain the ability to see more clearly...The circular relationship between observation and knowledge, and the way they feed each other...is the basis of any scientific career, and indeed the human condition that pushes us to make sense of the world."

DR. CAMILLA PANG
*Breakthrough*

Picture this: A team of software engineers, usually glued to their screens, are taken out of the office and dropped into the bustling streets of a foreign city. They're not there to code; they're there to watch, listen, and understand. Aidan, a researcher and friend of mine, knows that the only way to truly understand the needs of people her team is building software for is to see those needs firsthand. She arranged for the team to meet with small business owners—from barbers to booksellers—to see how their software was being used in real life. She once sent executives to Indonesia, riding on the backs of motorcycles in Jakarta so they could experience the chaos that delivery couriers faced, as a way of building empathy for the people the same executives were trying to attract to their platform. Another day, they were sitting in a makeshift workshop, watching as small business owners tried to use an app while juggling customers, payments, and appointments.

This is fieldwork in action—getting into the environment, seeing what people see, feeling what they feel. The engineers quickly realised that the challenges these small business owners faced were far more complex than anything they had imagined from their desks. It wasn't just about usability; it was about context, emotions, and the real-world messiness that no amount of office brainstorming could capture.

**Fieldwork is immersing yourself in the world of the problems you want to solve.** It's about observation—not from a distance, but up close and personal. It's the difference between theorising about how people do things and actually seeing it in action. It's messy, it's unpredictable, and it's incredibly powerful.

## THE ROLE OF OBSERVATION IN EXPERIMENTATION

The first step to bringing your ideas into the world is to understand the *landscape* they're about to enter. It sounds a little romantic, but it's true: your ideas exist within an environment, and if you don't know that environment well, you're essentially navigating without a map. Observation is your first opportunity to get out of your own head and into the real world—to move beyond your own perspective and see things as they truly are. It's the bedrock of any meaningful experimentation—watching, learning from real people in real places instead of your own assumptions. By observing, you can uncover the hidden needs, behaviours, and challenges that your idea should address. Think of observation as your way of seeing the whole puzzle before you start assembling the pieces. The process helps you anchor your ideas in reality. That's the power of observation. It brings clarity. It makes abstract problems tangible, and helps you see what matters.

## TWO APPROACHES: SHADOWING & EMULATING

There are two ways to observe: Shadowing (*watching*) and Emulating (*doing*.) Both are important, and each offers a different kind of lesson. Shadowing is about seeing and listening—gathering insights from the sidelines—while Emulating is about stepping into someone else's shoes to get a firsthand feel for an experience and environment. Shadowing helps you understand the what and where; emulating helps you understand the why.

# SHADOWING

Observation is about being present without interfering. It's about seeing things as they unfold naturally. No scripts, no prompts, just reality as it is. By watching things unfold in natural environments, you can start to see patterns, habits, and behaviours that tell you what's really going on. Are there *frustrations* that go unspoken? Are people finding *workarounds* that reveal an unmet need?

The key is to be a silent witness—to take it all in without judgement or preconceived ideas. For instance, if you're a writer, you might observe a bustling café, noting the subtle interactions. A raised eyebrow, a nervous smile. Small things that speak volumes about people's relationships and emotions. Observation allows you to see the small, often-overlooked details that can make a big difference.

Use this guide to record your observations during a shadowing session. And again—be careful to observe without influencing the environment.

| | |
|---|---|
| Setting | • Where are you observing?<br>• What is the context (e.g., busy café, workshop, office)? |
| People | • Who are you observing?<br>• What kind of roles or demographics do they represent? |
| Activities | • What are people doing?<br>• What actions or tasks stand out?<br>• Is there anything out of the ordinary? |
| Behaviours | • What do you notice about how people behave?<br>• Are there any repeated patterns, frustrations, or moments of flow? |
| Interactions | • How do people interact with tools, systems, or each other?<br>• Are there points of friction? |
| Unspoken Needs | • What workarounds, improvisations, or shortcuts do you notice?<br>• What might these suggest about unmet needs or pain points? |
| Key Insights | • What are the top insights you gained from this session?<br>• What questions do you have now that you didn't have at the beginning? |

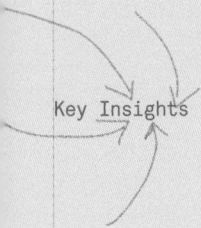

# EMULATING

Sometimes, watching isn't enough. To really understand something, you need to *experience it yourself*. By emulating the people and places you're trying to bring something new. This is where empathy comes into play. Emulation means stepping into someone else's shoes and living their experience to uncover the challenges, emotions, and barriers they face.

Imagine you were developing a product for busy parents. Instead of just observing them, you could spend a day emulating their routine: juggling work, cooking dinner, helping with homework. This firsthand experience gives you insights that observation alone might miss—like the stress of trying to finish a task while managing constant interruptions. Emulation helps you feel the friction points, which is invaluable in making sure you're creating something to fix a problem worth solving.

| | |
|---|---|
| Task or Role | • What are you emulating (e.g., using a product, performing a task, experiencing a journey or a 'life in the day')? |
| Challenges | • What was unexpectedly difficult?<br>• What specific steps caused frustration or confusion? |
| Successes | • What parts of the experience felt smooth or enjoyable?<br>• What made them work well? |
| Experience | • How did the process make you feel (e.g., overwhelmed, excited, annoyed)?<br>• What moments stood out emotionally? |
| Unmet Needs | • Were there moments where you needed support or tools that weren't available?<br>• What could have made the experience better? |
| Comparison to Observation | • How does your experience compare to what you observed (if applicable)?<br>• What new insights does this perspective give you? |
| Takeaways | • What are the top insights you gained from this session?<br>• What new questions do you have now that you didn't have at the beginning? |

## WHEN AND HOW TO USE BOTH APPROACHES

Observation and emulation work best together. Start by observing the *big picture*—how people behave, interact, and adapt in their natural environment. This will give you an understanding of the overall context. Once you have that foundation, dive deeper by emulating *specific experiences*. If you're designing a tool for frontline workers, watch them on the job to understand their environment, then try doing the work yourself to uncover the subtle, emotional layers of the experience.

Observation gives you objectivity; emulation adds empathy. By combining both, you gain a well-rounded understanding that makes your experiments more insightful.

## OBSERVE BEFORE YOU ACT

Observation isn't just the first step in the process—it's the foundation for everything that follows. Without it, you're guessing, relying on assumptions to fill in the gaps. And assumptions, no matter how well-intentioned, are blind spots waiting to trip you up. Observation gives you clarity. It helps you see not just the problems, but the patterns, the nuances, and the human realities that make those problems worth solving in the first place.

Think of it this way: observation is how you draw the map before setting out on the journey. It won't tell you exactly how to get where you're going, but it shows you the terrain—the barriers, the shortcuts, the uncharted paths. It gives you a sense of where to look, what to question, and where the opportunities might lie. The more time you spend observing, the more accurate that map becomes.

But here's the thing about observation: it doesn't just show you the obvious. It's in the quiet moments, the small details, the things people don't even realise they're revealing, that is where the real insights emerge. It's the barber juggling customers and payments while fumbling with an app that wasn't designed for his reality. It's the parent trying to finish a task while being interrupted for the third time in ten minutes. These moments don't shout—they whisper. And if you're not paying attention, you'll miss them.

Observation is also about humility. It asks you to set aside what you think you know and see the world as it really is. That can mean shadowing someone to understand their rhythms and challenges. Or it might mean emulating their experience—stepping into their shoes and feeling it for yourself. Both approaches matter, because they give you two things every good experiment needs: *objectivity* and *empathy*.

Here's what happens next. Once you've observed the landscape, you'll start to see patterns. Not everything will make sense right away, and that's fine. The point is to let the observations guide your next steps. What's worth testing? What questions still need answers? Observation doesn't hand you solutions, but it makes sure you're asking the right questions and that's how real progress begins.

One final tip. Before you move forward: Take one last look. Slow down. Observe again. Because the best ideas don't come from clever thinking alone. They come from seeing the world a little more *clearly* than you did before. That's the power of observation—it opens your eyes so the real work can begin.

# HYPOTHESISE *(Phase 2)*

# EDISON'S LIGHT BULB FILAMENT

In the fall of 1879, Thomas Edison stood in his lab surrounded by charred remnants of failed ideas. Carbonised paper, coconut fibre, strands of flax—all scorched, crumbled, and discarded in the pursuit of a single answer: What could burn long enough, bright enough, and reliably enough to light the world? He wasn't just inventing a light bulb; he was solving a problem that had stumped countless inventors before him. And he wasn't doing it with grand, sweeping strokes. He broke it down into small, bite-sized questions—a set of hypotheses. Every good *experiment* starts with a hypothesis specific enough to test on its own.

Each material Edison tested was its own experiment, its own tiny battle in the larger war of ideas. Would bamboo work? Maybe not. What about carbonised cardboard? Also no. Every test was a chance to learn—not just what failed, but why it failed. Edison's famous (and likely exaggerated) claim that he discovered "10,000 ways that won't work" isn't just a testament to his resilience. It's a window into his *process*. Failure wasn't the opposite of success—it was the raw material he needed to find it.

This relentless focus on iteration is what made Edison different. He didn't try to leap from darkness to brilliance in a single bound. Instead, he asked one small, testable question at a time. Will this hold up under heat? Can this conduct electricity?

Will this last long enough to be useful? These weren't sweeping, existential questions. They were practical, specific, and manageable. Each one brought him closer to the answer he needed, even when the answer was no.

Here's the thing: Edison didn't know bamboo would be the breakthrough material. What he did know was that by asking the *right questions*—questions he could test, refine, and learn from—he'd eventually stumble across the right answer. And he did. By the time he and his team landed on carbonised bamboo, they'd built not just a light bulb but a process and a way of thinking.

This story isn't about light bulbs. It's about how we tackle problems that feel too big to solve. Edison didn't get there because he was a genius (though I imagine he wasn't lacking in brains). He got there because he was patient and deliberate. He got there because he didn't fear failure. Most importantly, he got there because he understood the power of a good hypothesis—a small, focused question that moves you just one step closer to the solution.

That's where we'll begin: with the idea that every big breakthrough starts small. Each hypothesis is a chance to learn, to fail, to adjust, and to try again. The lesson isn't just in Edison's success—it's in the thousands of little failures that lit the way.

## BREAKING DOWN BIG PROBLEMS
## INTO SMALLER HYPOTHESES

In 1966, an ambitious idea flickered to life in the corridors of Britain's Ministry of Technology. What if, someone suggested, we could turn an entire town into the future? Slough, the Berkshire town 20 miles west of London, was to become a technological utopia, a laboratory for progress. Computers would hum in every office, advanced telecommunications would connect businesses like never before, and every gadget from the Ministry's arsenal would be unleashed in one monumental experiment. It would be, as the government envisioned, a model example of what could happen to the whole country.

Except it wasn't. *The Slough Experiment* never even got off the ground. Not because the technology didn't exist, but because the vision was too sprawling, too messy. There were no controls, no clear way to measure success. The experiment wasn't really an experiment—it was a wish list. Critics quickly piled on. Why spend public funds on an already prosperous part of the country? How would anyone know which interventions were working and which weren't? By the time the political bickering subsided, the idea had quietly disappeared, taking any potential lessons with it.

But here's the thing: the Slough Experiment teaches us as much in failure as Edison's light bulb does in success. It's a story about what happens when we try to do *too much* at once. Ambition, unchecked by focus, becomes its own undoing.

Now, think back to Edison. He wasn't short on ambition either, but his genius wasn't in dreaming big. It was in breaking big dreams down into small, testable parts. Instead of trying to invent the entire light bulb in one go, Edison asked, "What if we start with the filament? Which material might work best?" Every no brought him closer to the yes he needed. By isolating one variable at a time, he created experiments that taught him something, even when they failed.

The Slough Experiment, on the other hand, tried to tackle everything at once. In trying to modernise an entire town in a single sweep, with no way to track what was working and what wasn't, the entire effort was doomed. It's like trying to design a better car by simultaneously rethinking the engine, the tires, and the chassis without testing each part on its own. If it fails—and it probably will—it's going to be hard to know exactly why.

This is a cautionary tale. When you attempt too much, you learn almost nothing. Complex problems are rarely solved with grand, sweeping gestures. They're solved step by step, hypothesis by hypothesis, with each test narrowing the field of possibilities.

Edison's success and Slough's failure boil down to the same principle: focus. Edison focused on one question at a time, learning with each test. The Slough Experiment scattered its focus, learning nothing at all. It's not ambition that matters—it's clarity. The most ambitious ideas only succeed when they're broken down into clear, manageable questions. The truth is, the more you try to tackle at once, the less you actually understand.

# CRAFTING EFFECTIVE HYPOTHESES

**Focus on discrete, testable hypotheses, rather than a big, all-in endeavour.**

Big breakthroughs don't start with answers. They start with questions. But here's the catch: not all questions are created equal. The question "How do I change the world?" might feel inspiring, but it's impossible to answer. It's too broad, too abstract, and, let's be honest,—too overwhelming. The real magic happens when we take big, sprawling questions and transform them into something sharper, more concrete, and testable. That's what a good hypothesis does: it turns curiosity into clarity.

Let's return to Edison for a moment. He didn't sit down and ask, "How do I invent the light bulb?" That's not a hypothesis—it's a goal. Instead, he took that goal and broke it into questions he could actually answer. "What happens if I use carbonised paper for the filament?" "Will bamboo last longer than cotton thread?" Each question was specific. Each one could be tested. And with every test, he learned something—whether it worked or, more often, whether it didn't.

This process of taking an observation, framing it as a question, and turning it into a testable hypothesis isn't just for inventors. It's the foundation of any meaningful progress. And the best part is that it doesn't have to be complicated.

You don't need a lab or a team of scientists. You just need to ask the right kinds of questions. Let's break it down.

## START WITH AN OBSERVATION

Every hypothesis begins with curiosity. Edison noticed that some materials burned longer than others. Maybe you've noticed that customers hesitate at a particular step in your checkout process or that your team struggles with deadlines. Pay attention to those moments. It's where the best questions are born.

## FRAME THE QUESTION

Vague questions lead to vague results. Instead of asking, "Why don't customers check out faster?" ask, "What happens if we simplify the checkout form?" Instead "Why is the team missing deadlines?" ask, "Does breaking projects into weekly milestones make us more productive?" The key is to narrow your focus with a hunch or opinion. A good hypothesis is specific enough that you can prove it right or wrong.

## MAKE IT TESTABLE

A hypothesis isn't a statement of belief. It's a question you can test. Let's say you hypothesise that offering free shipping will increase sales. You can run a test where half of your customers see free shipping and the other half don't, then compare the results. If the data supports your hypothesis, great, you've learned something. If not, you've still learned something (your customers aren't driven to spend more if you offer free shipping.)

## DEFINE SUCCESS

Before you start testing, decide what success looks like. Edison's success metric for a filament was clear: it had to last long enough to make electric light practical. For your test, success might mean a 10% increase in sales, a 20% improvement in team efficiency, or any other measurable outcome. The point is to know what you're aiming for.

## KEEP IT SIMPLE

Here's where the Slough Experiment reminds us what not to do. If you try to test too many things at once, your results will be a mess. You'll never know if one thing leads to another with certainty. Test one thing at a time, and your results will actually mean something.

This is the art of turning a big, messy challenge into something manageable. Edison's genius wasn't in finding the perfect filament on his first try—it was in breaking the problem into hundreds of tiny experiments, each one designed to answer a single question. And here's the secret: you can do the same.

Take that big question you've been wrestling with. Break it into smaller ones. Then turn one of those smaller questions into a hypothesis you can test. You don't need to solve everything at once. You just need to find your first testable question and let it guide you. Because progress doesn't come from knowing all the answers. It comes from asking the right questions.

## STRUCTURING A TESTABLE HYPOTHESIS

At the heart of every successful experiment is a well-crafted hypothesis. Think of it as the anchor that keeps your test grounded and focused. A strong hypothesis clarifies what you're testing, why it matters, and what success will look like. This turns an idea into a something you can test. But first, you need to translate it into a clear plan. This plan should answer three fundamental questions:

1. What do you want to learn?
2. What signal will tell you it worked?
3. How will you measure success?

Your goal should be specific. Are you trying to understand customer behaviour? Test the effectiveness of a new process? Gauge audience reactions to a creative idea? Be clear about what you're investigating.

It also should have a clear measurable outcome. This could be engagement rates, completion times, or even subjective feedback. Your signal should align with the hypothesis and provide a clear yes or no answer. And finally, identify the metric that represents success. For example, if you're testing a new joke, your metric might be the number of laughs or the intensity of audience reaction. For a product, it might be how many people express a willingness to buy from you, or learn more about what you're offering.

| Hypothesis | "If I start my comedy set with a personal story, the audience will connect faster and laugh more." |
|---|---|
| Problem Context | Audiences can be slow to engage at the start of a set, which affects the energy for the rest of the performance. |
| Action | Open the set with a personal story that's relatable and humorous instead of a traditional observational joke. |
| Ideal Outcome | Audience engagement (measured by laughs and attentiveness) will improve within the first 2 minutes of the set. |
| Testing Variables | The type of opening (personal story vs. observational humor) and its impact on audience reaction. |
| Success Criteria | Success will be defined as a higher frequency of laughter and visible audience attentiveness (e.g., fewer distractions) in the first 2 minutes compared to previous sets. |
| Scope of the Test | Test the new opening over three performances in similar-sized venues with comparable audience demographics. |

## SETTING THE STAGE FOR PROTOTYPING

Prototyping is where ideas start to come to life. A good prototype is an experiment in action, and just like a good hypothesis, its purpose isn't to get everything right the first time. It's to learn. The stage for prototyping is set when your hypotheses are clear, your potential outcomes are documented, and your experiments are designed to answer specific, actionable questions.

But before you can test anything, you need to structure your approach. Think of it like crafting the blueprint for a building. Without a clear plan, you risk building walls where the doors should be or finding out the foundation can't hold the weight.

A prototype isn't the finished product—it's the physical embodiment of a hypothesis. It's a first draft. A way to test an idea in the real world. By structuring your hypothesis and experiment with discipline, you create a roadmap for learning something new. And that's the point.

Every experiment, whether it confirms your hypothesis or disproves it, moves you forward. So start small. Focus on one hypothesis. Test it. Learn from it. Then build on what you've learned. Because ingenuity rarely comes from a single, grand leap of faith—it's the sum of small incremental steps.

(Phase 3)

# PROTOTYPE

# 5,000 PROTOTYPES

For nearly a century, vacuum cleaners were nothing to write home about. They were big, clunky, and perfectly unremarkable—an accessory to chores. By the time James Dyson came along in the 1990s, they hadn't evolved much beyond the basics: pick up dirt, dump it out, repeat. Yet Dyson saw something no one else did. He didn't see just a vacuum. He saw an opportunity to revolutionise an industry people barely thought about.

Dyson didn't arrive at his groundbreaking, bagless cyclone vacuum overnight. He didn't even get there after 100 tries. Reportedly, he built over 5,000 *prototypes* before he nailed it. Imagine how many evenings he spent tinkering, failing, reworking, and failing again. Each prototype wasn't just a step forward; it was a question. What happens if I change this? Will it work better if I tweak that? Every iteration brought him closer to something extraordinary.

Dyson is an example of the power of prototyping. It's a reminder that before we can get to the polished, finished version of anything, we need to get messy. A prototype isn't meant to be *perfect*. It's a tool for thinking, testing, and learning. It's where ideas stop being ideas and start becoming something real.

Here's the secret: there's no single way to prototype. Some prototypes are *evolutionary*, like Dyson's vacuums, refined over time, inching closer to the final version. Others are *disposable*, quick sketches or mock-ups meant to answer a single question and then thrown away. Both types are useful, depending on the problem you're trying to solve. But what they share is a common goal: to teach you something.

Prototyping is about exploring possibilities without going all-in. Taking an idea, giving it form, and then testing it to see what works. And when it doesn't work (which it often won't at first) the feedback you receive is still valuable. The prototype that breaks, flops, or misses the mark can be just as important as the one that succeeds.

And this is where the art of prototyping truly shines. It's not just about building; it's about why you're building. Prototypes can serve different purposes, depending on where you are in the process or what you're trying to achieve. Dyson's journey highlights just one of those paths. Let's break it down further.

## PROTOTYPE TO EXPLORE

Sometimes, the goal isn't to solve a specific problem but to imagine what's possible, to dream big without restrictions. It's where you explore even the most audacious ideas, leaving the question of feasibility for later. If you explore in a more free way first, you'll have a guiding vision for thinking and iteratively more practically later.

## PROTOTYPE TO LEARN

Prototyping to learn shifts the focus from your ideas to the people and places you're making it for. It's about discovering what people want and need, their actions, and the kinds of choices they'll make. These prototypes are all about mimicking an experience or idea, often manually, to learn how people respond to and engage with it. The aim is to experiment on the key building blocks of the concept to check whether or not they are solving real problems in the right way.

## PROTOTYPE TO MEASURE

Finally, prototyping to measure is about validation. It's where you test how much an idea resonates, solves a problem, or is worth further investment. Here, you're gauging demand, comparing versions, or seeing how well it connects with people or solves a problem. It's like a shortcut to knowing whether something is worth dedicating more time and effort, or not.

# PINK HAT PROTOTYPE

# PINK HAT PROTOTYPING

## Thinking without constraints

A Pink Hat Prototype is the most ambitious vision of an idea, in full, and as if there are no constraints. Named after the idea of putting on a metaphorical 'magic pink hat' to permit unbounded possibilities. Here the focus is to imagine and the best possible version of an idea, no matter how impractical or impossible it may initially seem. The goal isn't feasibility, it's inspiration. By giving shape to a vision, you'll be creating something to inform more realistic iterations in the future.

For instance, imagine you're designing a new public transit system. A Pink Hat version might include self-driving pods that arrive on demand. You might imagine a network of trains that adapt their routes based on the needs of people onboard, skipping or adding stops as needed. While some elements might go beyond what's possible today, they still serve as an inspirational nudge towards reshaping what's possible.

### Example

A fashion designer might create a Pink Hat Prototype by sketching an avant-garde collection made entirely from bioluminescent fabrics, envisioning a world where clothing is both functional and luminous. While some elements might remain fantastical, others—like integrating light-reactive materials—could become the seeds of future, feasible designs.

Everything is a Prototype

Experimentation

Not to mention, the starting point of something that could be prototyped more tangibly right now.

## Practical Tip

Try combining Pink Hat Prototyping with grounded methods like Wizard of Oz or Frankenstein Prototyping to explore how aspirational ideas can inform more practical solutions.

## Challenges

**Unrealistic Expectations:** There's a risk of becoming too attached to ideas that are unfeasible in the short term. Think of a Pink Hat Prototype as a source of inspiration, not a detailed blueprint.

**Skepticism:** Skepticism is a common reaction when bold ideas are introduced, especially when they seem impossible or ambitious at first glance. Present the prototype as the beginning of something, an exploration of possibilities, not a finished plan.

**Translating Dreams into Reality:** Moving from the dream to actionable steps can feel overwhelming. Use your Pink Hat Prototype to identify which elements are most compelling and explore ways to achieve them incrementally.

# INSTRUCTIONS

## 1. Define the Ultimate Vision

What's the most extraordinary, idealised version of your concept? Think about how it would look, feel, or function in a perfect world. What kind impact do you want it to have? What it would achieve if there were no limits?

## 2. Dream Boldly

Gather your team (or yourself) and imagine without constraints. Embrace the wild, impossible, and impractical. This is the time to dream big. Ask: What's the "pink hat" version of this idea? If there were no limitations—money, technology, time—what would you create?

## 3. Visualise

Turn your ideas into something tangible. Draw a detailed sketch, create a short video, or make a physical model. Use storytelling to paint a vivid picture.

## 4. Share and Narrate

Present your Pink Hat Prototype in any way that tells its story. Use visuals or even role-playing to immerse people.

## 5. Reflect and Extract

Ask yourself and others: Which elements of this vision resonate the most? Are there parts of this dream that could be adapted or achieved in the short term? What does this tell us about what's truly important for the idea?

# FRANKENSTEIN

*Prototype to Explore*

# FRANKENSTEIN PROTOTYPES

## Test the feasibility of new ideas by using parts of what already exists

Frankenstein Prototyping is when you combine parts of existing things to make and explore something new. Inspired by Dr. Frankenstein's approach of assembling different parts to bring something to life, this method demands a level of resourcefulness and hackiness—taking what's available to build a working version of an idea. It's not about achieving a polished result but about creating something functional that can be experienced, tested, and refined. As a method, it's a useful way to validate something for its functionality when you're not yet ready to invest in developing anything bespoke or expensive. It allows you to evaluate if a concept has potential before diving in head first.

## Example

Suppose you want to create a prototype of a portable workstation for your home. Rather than creating custom components, you pull together what you have around. An old folding table, adjustable clamps, the tablet holder from a car, and a cushioned chair. You then combine these elements to test comfort, usability, and adaptability. It's not sleek, but you can explore whether the idea works before investing more time and resources towards making it entirely from scratch.

## Practical Tip

Use whatever you can find. Be open to using a range of items, parts, or hacks. The key to Frankenstein Prototyping is to quickly put things together to test functionality, regardless of it being perfect or pretty.

## Challenges

**Instability:** Frankenstein Prototypes are inherently rough, often made from mismatched parts that don't fit perfectly together. The focus is on proving the core idea works. If something wobbles or doesn't fit quite right, that's fine at this stage.

**Messy Components:** Not everything you use will work smoothly together. Embrace the rough edges. Adjust, swap out, or jerry-rig elements as needed to see what's viable for your next iteration.

# INSTRUCTIONS

## 1. Identify the Core Challenge

Define the basic functionality you want to test. What problem are you trying to solve, or what experience do you want to create?

## 2. Gather Available Components

Collect existing items you have access to that could work as component pieces. Be rough. Repurpose tools, parts, or household items that could fit your needs.

## 3. Assemble the Prototype

Use the different parts to create a working version of your concept. This stage is all about combining components, even if, in the real world, that means using tape, screws, or improvised supports to make them work together.

## 4. Test its Functionality

Use your Frankenstein Prototype in real scenarios to understand if it works. Take notes on usability, convenience, or areas that need improvement. What works? What doesn't?

## 5. Edit and Iterate on the Fly

Based on your testing, tweak and adjust the prototype. Identify what parts work well together and where you need to refine the idea or explore different components.

# WIZARD OF OZ

*Prototype to Learn*

# WIZARD OF OZ

## Test complex ideas with minimal resources

Wizard of Oz Prototyping is a method where someone interacts with what appears to be a fully functioning system, but behind the scenes, a human is manually making it happen. This approach is particularly useful when trying to build things that are complex or would take a lot of time and resources to make the first version, allowing you to validate without needing to develop the full idea. The name comes from The Wizard of Oz film, where the great and powerful wizard is actually just a person behind a curtain pulling levers.

Wizard of Oz Prototyping helps you test ideas, observe people's behaviour, and understand what features or interactions are most valuable. All without needing to invest time and money in building something which might turn out to be wrong or flawed in the first place. Essentially, it's a way of faking the experience to see if it's worth pursuing.

## Example
Imagine you're prototyping a new voice assistant that helps people manage their weekly schedules. Instead of building the entire system and hoping for the best, you create a Wizard of Oz prototype. In one room, you set up a microphone and speaker and tell people they are about to test a new voice-activated technology. Behind the scenes in another room,

Experimentation

a person listens to the requests and responds as if they are the system, essentially faking it. This allows you to observe how people interact with the assistant, e.g. what kinds of questions they ask, how they respond to answers, and what expectations they have. By simulating the functionality with a human operator, you gain critical insights into which features are must-haves and which are unnecessary, before committing to the full project.

## Practical Tip

To ensure a seamless experience, have a set of common tasks you might need to perform prepared ahead of time. This makes it easier for the 'wizard' behind the scenes to maintain consistency and avoid hesitation, keeping the illusion of an automated system intact.

## Challenges

**Maintaining the Illusion:** People might realise there's a person behind the curtain, breaking the "magic" of their experience. Carefully plan and rehearse interactions to keep the illusion intact, and ensure the operator is well-prepared to respond quickly and naturally.

**Scalability Issues:** Manually operating a system behind the scenes is labour-intensive and can't be scaled easily. Use Wizard of Oz Prototypes for specific scenarios or early testing phases to determine if something is worth pursuing, particularly if it's going to be laborious or expensive.

# INSTRUCTIONS

## 1. Define the Goal

Decide what you want to learn. Are you looking to understand behaviour, test a specific part of an idea, or validate a concept?

## 2. Create a Mock Interface

Develop a fake of the system you're simulating. It could be a screen interface, a voice command setup, or even a mock device. Make it as realistic, and believable, as possible.

## 3. Script the Interactions

Prepare scripts or outline potential interactions. Think through what people are likely to say or do and how the system (i.e., the "wizard" behind the scenes) should respond.

## 4. Assign a Wizard

Have someone be "the system", responding to requests or actions. This person needs to be familiar with the scripts and able to respond naturally to things that aren't pre-prepared.

## 5. Test with Real People

Observe their behaviour, gather feedback, and pay close attention to how they respond to different aspects of what you're simulating. Are they confused at any point? Which things do they gravitate towards?

## 6. Analyse and Iterate

Review the data gathered during the test. What worked well? What felt unnatural or confused people? Use these insights to refine your concept before moving on or testing again.

# CONCIERGE

*Prototype to Learn*

# CONCIERGE PROTOTYPING

## Simulate something manually to learn through experience

Concierge Prototyping is a method where you manually deliver a 'service' to a small group of people, simulating an idea as if it already existed. Unlike other prototyping methods, Concierge Prototypes put a strong focus on understanding someone's journey over time and refining over time with changes in how you act as the 'concierge.' This method allows you to test the viability of your idea and validate whether it's something people truly need by playing the role yourself.

In a Concierge Prototype, you're essentially acting as the service yourself. By manually guiding people through different moments, you gain a deeper understanding of their pain points, preferences, and needs.

## Example

Imagine you're developing some kind of digital shopping tool.Instead of building it right away, you act as a personal shopper. You meet with people to understand their tastes, research items based on their preferences, purchase products for them, and then deliver the curated selection in person. Throughout this process, you document each interaction— learning what they value most and where the friction lies.

This manual version of your service helps you identify which parts are worth automating and which features aren't needed at all.

## Practical Tip

Focus on the experience. Concierge Prototyping allows you to immerse yourself in the experience of an idea by playing the role of the idea itself. Document each step and note what works well and what causes frustration. The things you'll learn are invaluable for refining the idea, and providing not just if it's worthwhile, but also the key elements it should have, and what it can go without.

## Challenges

**Time-Consuming:** Playing the 'concierge' is labour-intensive and not manageable in the long term. Focus on delivering the service to a small, representative group. The goal isn't to serve a large audience at scale. Instead, it's to learn from the experience and collect insights on the good, the bad, and the unexpected.

**Limited Scalability:** The personalised, hands-on nature of a Concierge Prototype doesn't easily translate to a broader group of people. Treat this method as an early learning phase. Use it to uncover what's essential and what's not, so if you keep going, you do so with real understanding and experience, not assumptions.

# INSTRUCTIONS

## 1. Identify the Core Service

Determine what core service or product offering you want to test. What's the essence of what you're trying to deliver?

## 2. Recruit a Small Group of People

Select a small, manageable group of people to test the service. They should be representative of your intended audience to provide the most relevant insights.

## 3. Deliver the Service Manually

Act as the service yourself. For example, imagine you're testing a subscription-based meal delivery service You could personally curate and deliver the products. Document each action you take, how people respond, and any issues or questions that come up along the way.

## 4. Gather Feedback

Observe how people interact with you, the 'service.' Ask questions and gather feedback to understand what they enjoy, what they find frustrating, and what they feel is missing.

## 5. Iterate on the Process

Use the feedback and observations to refine as you go. What can be streamlined or improved? This is essential for knowing the difference between the must-have's, nice-to-have's, and what you can ignore.

# FRONT DOOR TEST

*Prototype to Measure*

# FRONT DOOR TEST

## Gauge if something resonates by testing it in its rawest form

A Front Door Prototype is a way of presenting the "first touch" of your idea or offering in its simplest, most digestible form to test whether people are interested or not. This could take the shape of a landing page, a sign-up sheet, a free sample, or any form of a "minimal viable experience." The goal is to test how many people metaphorically—or literally—step through your front door, signalling interest in what lies beyond. It reduces the risk of investing in something that might not resonate, while also helping you identify early fans, supporters, or customers.

Imagine opening a café. Instead of setting up the whole venue, you could start by offering coffee samples on the sidewalk to see if passersby are intrigued. Their willingness to try your coffee—and their feedback—can help you decide whether to open a full store in that location.

A Front Door Prototype is less about perfecting the entire offering and more about finding out if there's enough interest or appetite to take the next step. It's a test of the core idea: **Does this resonate with people?**

## Example

A Front Door Prototype can take the form of the first chapter of a book that is shared on a blog or via a mailing list. The engagement of readers (downloads, feedback, requests for more, etc.) helps the author decide whether the book is worth writing in full, or if it's something to abandon in exchange for another project.

## Practical Tip

Keep it simple. You don't need to showcase every detail or feature of an idea. Instead, focus on creating curiosity and demonstrating the core value of the concept.

## Challenges

**Too Much Information:** Providing too much upfront can overwhelm or confuse people. Focus on clarity. Boil your concept down to one sentence, one page, or a single image that captures its essence.

**Too Little Information:** If your prototype has too little detail, people might not understand its purpose or potential value. Strike a balance. Use clear, concise language or visuals that convey the idea without oversharing.

# INSTRUCTIONS

### 1. Identify Your Goal

What do you want to learn from this test? Are you gauging general interest, specific preferences, or willingness to engage? Define your objectives clearly.

### 2. Create the Front Door

Develop a preview or short demo. This could be a flyer or poster, a single web page with a sign-up form, or a sample product or experience.

### 3. Highlight the Value

Craft a clear, compelling message that communicates why someone should care. Ask yourself: What's the benefit or unique appeal?

### 4. Offer a Simple Call to Action (CTA)

Give people a way to express interest. This might include: Signing up for updates, pre-ordering, or providing feedback.

### 5. Track Engagement

Pay attention to how people respond. This will give you a tangible idea of the level of interest.

### 6. Analyse the Results

Review the data you've gathered. Did enough people respond positively to justify moving forward? What specific feedback stands out?

# HEAD TO HEAD

*Prototype to Measure*

# HEAD TO HEAD

**Comparing two versions of an idea to determine which one is better.**

A Head to Head (or A/B Test as it's often known) is when you create a way to compare two options to find out which one works better. Whether it's testing two versions of a recipe, two formats for a presentation, or two layouts for a garden, this method lets you learn by comparing the feedback or data you can capture.

The simpler the comparison the better. Imagine you're trying to decide on the best recipe for a menu in a restaurant, and the only difference between two options is that one uses chicken while the other uses lamb. If people are ordering more of the chicken, or the feedback the floor staff are receiving is more positive, you would easily be able to attribute it to the difference in protein. But be warned: It can be tempting to make two versions of something so different that, even when there's a clear winner, you won't be able to know exactly why. Therefore, keep it as simple as possible.

A Head to Head can also be used iteratively over time. If customers raved about the chicken option and ordered it more than the lamb, that doesn't necessarily mean the test is over. You could try duck, venison, or vegetarian options. You could also leave the chicken and start to experiment with different sides and sauces. In theory, it could go on forever. It's up to you when to stop. Continue to iterate and compare as possible, but keep an eye on when the feedback between two options (and which is the clear winner) becomes difficult to see. You might be nearing the end of where a Head to Head is useful, or there's any sizable improvements to be made.

### Example

A non-profit organisation might use Head to Head to test different approaches to engage with donors to raise more money.

### Practical Tip

Focus on testing one variable at a time to ensure results are clear and actionable.

### Challenges

To get meaningful results, you want your sample size to be large enough and you want to run the test for a good length of time. But that doesn't mean it needs the rigor of academic research or statistical significance. It's about leaving the test to run for long enough to begin seeing patterns, trends, and clusters of repeatable results.

# INSTRUCTIONS

## 1. Decide What You're Testing

What's the one thing you want to evaluate? (e.g. the best protein in a recipe.)

## 2. Create Two Variations

**Version A (Control):** The standard or existing approach. If it's not something that already exists, that's OK, it can still be the control.
**Version B (Variation):** A modified or new approach that introduces a specific change.

## 3. Divide Your Audience 50/50

Split the people you're going to test with evenly between the two groups. (e.g. half of the tables in the restaurant get a menu with the chicken option, and the other half get a menu with lamb.) If you can't do it, then expose Version A and Version B to similiar people and environments on separate occasions.

## 4. Measure What Matters

This can be direct measures (e.g. number of orders for Version A vs. Version B) or indirect measures (e.g. verbal feedback from customers, size of the tip left at the end of the meal, etc.)

## 5. Review the Results

Compare the results of both versions and decide which one performed better. If there's no clear difference, it could be that you need to let the test happen for longer (e.g. more than one night in the restaurant). If that doesn't change anything, then there's no clear winner. Maybe the real winner is letting the customer choose which protein they want from a number of options when they order.

*(Phase 4)*
# TEST

# A WAY OF SEEING

Testing is where ideas leave the safe confines of your imagination and collide with *reality*. And while this might sound like a moment of judgement, it's much more than that. Testing is about learning and paying attention to what you didn't expect, watching how your ideas perform, and finding ways to refine them. Testing isn't the end of the journey—it's an extension of observation. Only this time, the world is observing you.

Testing shouldn't confirm what you already know or hoped was true. It should reveal something new. To answer: What happens when your prototype meets its first real audience? Does it work the way you intended? Is it better, worse, or just as expected? Testing is where those questions become answers.

## FINDING FOCUS AND CLARITY

One of the biggest mistakes people make in testing is trying to do *too much* at once. The goal isn't to validate an entire concept—it's to isolate and answer one specific question. Think of Thomas Edison and his light bulb. He didn't lump together every problem and tried to test them all at once. He broke the challenge into smaller, manageable pieces—first testing different materials one at a time to find the one that worked best for the filament.

Your approach to testing should follow the same principle: focus. Ask yourself: What is the one thing I need to *learn* from this test? What *evidence* will tell me if my idea is working or not? What can I observe that might reveal something *unexpected*?

For example, imagine you were creating a new workshop format. You wouldn't test the entire new format in one go. You would start small: Testing just the opening exercise. Does it engage participants the way you hoped? Does it prime them for the rest of the workshop? The more specific the focus of your test, the more conclusive and actionable the insights will be.

## WHERE TO TEST: FINDING THE RIGHT ENVIRONMENT AND PEOPLE

Testing isn't just about *what* you test—it's about *where* you test it. The environment you choose shapes the results you'll get, so it's important to think carefully about where your prototype will be exposed to people in the world.

Consider the German town of Haßloch (Hassloch), the 'perfectly average German city'. Haßloch has been used for years as a test ground by researchers to experiment. It's the perfect place to evaluate how a product will do in Germany as a whole because the demographics of the town closely mirror national averages, therefore the behaviours and reactions of 20,000 people in Haßloch are signals of what you can expect across the entire country. In 2014, roughly one third of households were taking part in some kind of a test, be it the advertisements they saw on television or products on the shelves of the supermarket.

The advice is straightforward: Pick an environment or group that *mirrors* your target audience as much as possible. The results of your tests won't generalise if your testing ground is too niche. If it's too broad, you may lose the nuance that makes your work special. The perfect testing environment is a balance: representative enough to give you valuable insights but focused enough that you can make sense of the feedback and data you collect.

When creating your test environment, consider:

- **Participants:** Who are the *people* engaging with your prototype? Are they the right audience for what you're testing? (Hint: it's not always your biggest fans or closest peers. They might skew the results.)
- **Context:** Does the *environment* reflect how this prototype will eventually be used? For example, testing a comedy set at an open mic will give you a very different read than performing for a corporate audience.
- **Biases:** Be mindful of biases. There are many, but two of the most common to watch out for are confirmation bias (only seeing what confirms your assumptions) and availability bias (overemphasising the most obvious or recent feedback). The environment should help you stay open to unexpected insights, not just reinforce what you already think.

Testing isn't just about proving whether an idea works or not. It's a *mindset*. A way of seeing how your ideas interact with the real world. It's about uncovering what you couldn't predict, finding *clarity* in what you find, and setting up the next step with more insight than you had before.

For example, if the first joke in a new standup comedy routine doesn't land: Was it you? Was it the content? Was it the delivery? Was it the audience? It might have worked in rehearsal, but it didn't survive a real crowd. So, what does that tell you about how to improve? Every test should make you a little bit smarter about what to do next.

Like Edison, chances are you won't get the results you hoped for, be it the first try or the tenth. But the value of testing isn't in perfect results. It's in the questions it answers, the *surprises* it reveals, and the new questions it inspires. So, test your ideas. Observe what happens. Learn. And then test again. Progress might not be predictable. But it is built from every insight, pivot, and unexpected lesson along the way.

5

# ITERA
# TION

*From Feedback to Progress*

# REAL PROGRESS

We love the idea of a breakthrough. The 'aha' moment. A flash of brilliance. The feeling of everything clicking into place. But breakthroughs, if they happen at all, are rare. And even when they do, they're usually just the tip of the iceberg. Beneath them lies the actual work: The grinding, patient, and unglamorous beats of iteration after iteration. It's not flashy or dramatic. It rarely gets the recognition it deserves. But it's where progress happens.

Take Maree, for example. As a first-time children's book author, she poured her heart into her manuscript. Every character was personal, every line a reflection of her values. When she handed her draft to an editor, she hoped for validation. Maybe even a little praise. Instead, she got the kind of feedback that feels like a punch to the gut. The characters were flat. The story lacked tension. The editor wasn't just critiquing her book; it felt like they were critiquing her.

Her first instinct was defensiveness. She wanted to explain her choices, to push back, to say, "You just don't get it." And yet, somewhere in that difficult process, Maree began to listen. She stopped seeing the feedback as an attack and started seeing it as an invitation. What if the editor was right? What if the story could be stronger, the characters more alive? With every rewrite, Maree chipped away at the weaknesses in her manuscript. She rewrote, reimagined, reshaped. Slowly and painstakingly, the story came to life. And in the end, it wasn't just her book that changed. She did too.

Iteration is like that. It's not about grand gestures or sweeping changes. It's about the small, deliberate steps that bring you closer to where you want to be. Each step builds on the last, laying down lessons, sharpening ideas, and revealing things you couldn't have seen at the start. It's not always comfortable, and it's rarely easy. But it's what turns a good idea into a great one—and, sometimes, a great idea into a breakthrough.

Modern culture tends to glorify *outcomes*. The bestselling book. The award-winning product. What's often forgotten is that every one of those successes is built on a thousand small steps. Each draft, each test, and each iteration gets us a little closer. Iteration isn't about being right the first time; it's about being willing to try again and again until it's as good as it can be.

Here's the thing: iteration isn't just for inventors, authors, or entrepreneurs. It's for anyone trying to make something better. Whether it's a project, a process, or themselves. It's about showing up, paying attention, and letting go of the need to be perfect. Because there's no such thing as perfect. There's only a better next version.

As we go over how to iterate, remind yourself of the message littered throughout this book: progress doesn't come from one big leap forward. It comes from a series of small, deliberate steps. It's about listening, learning, and being open to feedback and change. Iteration is messy and humbling. And it's powerful—not just because it improves what we make, but because it transforms how we see the world and ourselves.

So let's begin, not by aiming for perfection, but by looking for what could be better. Progress doesn't wait for the perfect plan. It happens in a loop of trying, learning, adjusting, and trying again. That's how extraordinary things get done, one imperfect step at a time.

## TURNING FEEDBACK INTO ACTION

So you've gathered feedback on your prototype, initial version of an idea, or a first draft of something. Maybe some of it was what you expected. Maybe some of it wasn't. Now comes the hard part: making sense of what you've learned and deciding what to do next. Closing the loop isn't just about receiving feedback. It's about figuring out which insights will push you forward and which ones to set aside.

The goal of this stage is clarity. Not every piece of feedback will lead to action, and not every adjustment will be the right one. The key is to step back, reflect, and determine: What's the single most important thing to focus on next?

Iteration is about doing less, not more. Instead of trying to fix every flawed assumption or misunderstanding all at once, focus on one change that you think will make the biggest difference—then test again.

## MAKING SENSE OF FEEDBACK

The feedback you've gathered is only as useful as what you do with it. Before diving in, take a moment to interrogate the results:

- **What did the feedback confirm?** Did it validate part of your hypothesis or prototype? What worked, and why or why not?
- **What surprised you?** Did the results reveal something unexpected? These surprises are often where the nuggets of insights lie.
- **What didn't work?** Look for patterns in what people struggled with or misunderstood. Are these issues deal-breakers, or can they be refined?
- **What's actionable?** Not all feedback is worth acting on.
- **Ask:** Which changes will move me closer to my goal?

For example, if your hypothesis was that a personal story would make your comedy set more engaging, and the feedback shows that while the story worked, it ran too long and lost momentum, your next step isn't to scrap the story entirely, it's to refine it. Feedback helps you decide what parts of the story to:

- **Keep:** Things that work well.
- **Tweak:** Things that show promise but need adjustment.
- **Scrap:** Things that don't serve a purpose or are wrong.

Your prototype is like a rough sculpture. You're not starting over each time—you're chiselling away at the edges, refining the form with each pass. If a joke worked well in your comedy set but it was too long, your next iteration should be shorter. You don't need to scrap it entirely.

## PREPARING THE NEXT ITERATION

Finishing a single test doesn't mean finishing for good. It means preparing the next experiment that builds on what you've learned. Every iteration brings you closer to the best possible version of the idea. Here's how to stay on track:

- **Document what you learned:** Write down what worked, what didn't, and what questions remain. This will guide your next steps and keep you from repeating the same mistakes again.
- **Set a goal for the next iteration:** What's the one thing you want to improve or test next?
- **Refine the hypothesis:** How would you change your hunch or assumption based on what you've learned?
- **Adjust the prototype:** Make changes to the part of the prototype connected to the feedback.
- **Move forward:** Progress happens in motion, not in endless reflection. Don't get stuck trying to perfect this stage.
- **Test Again (and Again):** Take your revised hypothesis or prototype, and seek out more feedback. This isn't a new experiment. It's the next step in the same process. You're testing the same idea, but with focused adjustments based on what you've learned. Do it repeatedly.

## ITERATING ON A JOKE

Let's return to the example of a comedian testing a personal story as the opening to their standup set:

- **Feedback:** Audiences found the story engaging but said it felt too long. Some audience members mentioned that the punchline landed well, but the setup dragged.
- **What to Keep:** The story itself is good. It grabs people's attention and establishes a connection.
- **What to Tweak:** Shorten the setup. Find ways of trimming the time it takes to tell the story.
- **What to Scrap:** Cut unnecessary details that don't serve the punchline.
- **Next Iteration Goal:** Test the shortened version in the next two performances and see if the audience responds better than the previous iteration.

The comedian isn't throwing out the entire experiment. They're running the same test again, but with adjustments designed to address the pacing issues and highlight the punchline's impact.

Feedback isn't a final verdict. It's more like a compass pointing you in the direction of what to do next. Each iteration is one step closer to the best version of whatever it is you're working on. But it's up to you to take the next step.

Iteration is how you get better, safely and incrementally. And that's how meaningful progress happens—one small improvement at a time. You don't have to accept every piece of feedback or data, but you do have to be open to the possibility that there's something to learn from it—especially when it's hard to hear.

THIS BOOK IS A PROTOTYPE

A GUIDE TO MAKING
BETTER MISTAKES

The earliest record of the project that
became this book. Circa mid-2020.

# END NOTE

"The saddest thing in life is wasted talent, and the choices that you make will shape your life forever."

CHAZZ PALMINTERI

As I sit here, fingers on the keyboard, I'm struck by the irony of finishing a book about creativity while feeling stuck in the very process I'm trying to champion. Writing this book wasn't a smooth journey. There were days when every sentence felt wrong, when I rewrote paragraphs only to delete them again, and when doubt whispered, "Who are *you* to write this?"

This book has had three major title changes, countless subtitle revisions, and rounds upon rounds of edits. At one point, I had convinced myself it might never exist. I've worked with two literary agents, sent proposals into the void, and faced rejections from every publisher you can imagine. Each rejection chipped away at my confidence, but somehow, every one of them also built something—grit, perspective, and clarity about why this book mattered to me.

Through all the ups and downs, I've realized that writing this book wasn't just an act of creation. It was an act of prototyping. Testing ideas, discarding drafts, trying again—it mirrored the very processes I've described in these pages. And while the journey felt humbling, messy, and uncertain, it also reminded me of why this work matters.

When I began writing, I set out to answer a few big questions: Why do so many of us hold back from pursuing our ideas? How can we approach challenges more confidently and with less fear? What does it take to shift from dreaming about what's possible to actually making it happen?

These questions have shaped every chapter, story, and tool I've shared with you. From Jack's rigid bakery dream to Lisa's adaptable experiments, from the kindergarteners who fail fearlessly to the researchers who decode human ingenuity, we've explored the mindset and methods behind better ideas and better mistakes.

But as I wrote, I realised that these weren't just questions for you; they were questions for me, too. I didn't write this book as someone who's mastered every step, but as someone who's fumbled along, learning the same lessons over and over again. It's been a journey of testing, failing, and iterating—a messy act of creativity. This book, like everything, is a prototype too.

This book hasn't just been about learning to prototype; it's about becoming more *Experimental*. It's about embracing the mindset that sees every challenge, failure, or setback as part of the process. It's about showing up with curiosity and courage, even when the path ahead isn't clear.

To the people whose work and research I've mentioned, thank you for showing me what persistence looks like in practice. To the friends, colleagues, and mentors who listened patiently when I was stuck, who read early drafts and asked questions that cut straight to the heart: Your generosity gave this book life. Your belief in the value of these ideas carried me when my own belief faltered.

And finally, to you, the reader: thank you for picking up this book. Whether it met you in a moment of inspiration or uncertainty, I hope it's given you something to take with you: Questions to explore, the courage to keep going, or even the comfort of knowing you're not alone in the messiness of creating and evolving something new. At worst, I hope it's the right size and shape to fill a void on a shelf or hold a door ajar.

So here we are at the end. Or the next beginning. I hope the ideas in this book have sparked something for you—a hypothesis, a possibility, or even just the reassurance that it's okay to be a work in progress. If you take one thing from these pages, let it be this: progress isn't about perfection; it's about showing up for the next step and the one after that.

I'm still iterating and trying to figure it all out. But if I've learned anything, it's this: the moments when you feel the most stuck are often right before a breakthrough.

Thank you for following along. The next step is yours.

Dear Brendan,

Thanks for getting in touch with us and introducing us to your project 'Deciding in the Dark'. We've discussed your project here and looked at your proposal, also considering your offer to experiment with the format. However we don't think that the project and publication would be a right fit with ████████████████

I understand you're searching for a publisher outside of traditional big publishers. One publisher that came to mind, who is not traditional in that sense, but might be a better fit than us, ██████████████

We wish you the best of luck with the publication.

---
Best,
████████████

Editor | ████████████████

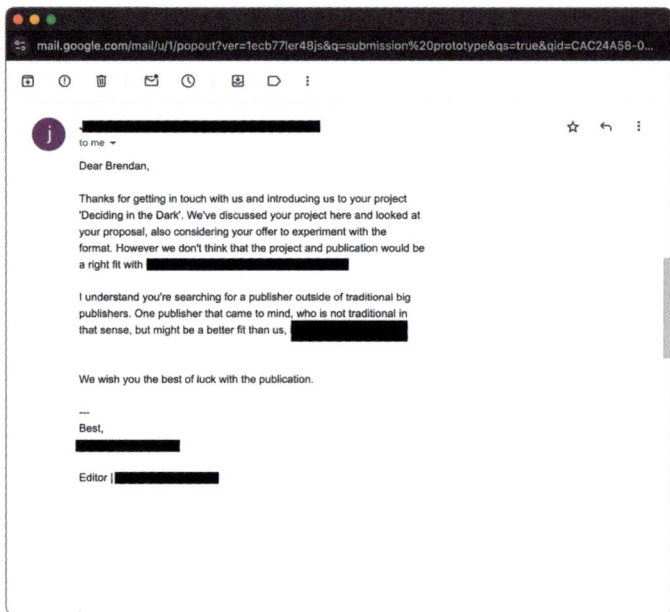

One of many rejections. Or perhaps just feedback to shape the next iteration...

# ACKNOWLEDGEMENTS

While my name is the only one on the cover, this book is the result of the hard work and insights of many extraordinary people. Any shortcomings are mine alone, but any success is shared with all those who helped bring this project to life. I owe each of you a profound debt of gratitude.

To Kate Evans at PFD, my first agent, who took a hyperbolic proposal from an unknown voice and shaped it into something focused and compelling—thank you for your vision, patience, and persistence. We nearly got there. To Euan Thorneycroft at A.M. Heath, who, despite the project being a dead horse, gave it the time of day to see if it still had legs—thank you for your openness and encouragement. To my publisher, Harm, and the team at BIS, thank you for your faith and patience. I'm sorry I still don't fully grasp the concept of a deadline.

To Joanne, Montana, and James, your aesthetic and invaluable advice gave this project personality and polish. To Jacqui and Maria, who edited patiently over many painful iterations—thank you for your sharp eyes and thoughtful contributions. To Lisa O'Brien, whose feedback over drinks in the book's formative days, hype throughout, and kindness in the final hours kept me motivated and grounded—thank you.

And finally, to everyone who read early drafts, offered feedback, or simply cheered me on when I needed it most—this book is as much yours as it is mine.

Any references to third-party content or published works are the copyright of their respective owners.